THE
CONSTITUTION
Made Easy

WE, the People of the United States, in order to form

a more perfect union, to establish justice, insure domestic tranquility, provide for the common defence, promote the general welfare, and secure the blessings of liberty to ourselves and our posterity, do ordain and establish this Constitution for the United States of America.

ARTICLE I.

Sect. 1. ALL legislative powers herein granted shall be vested in a Congress of the United States, which shall consist of a Senate and House of Representatives.

Sect. 2. The House of Representatives shall be composed of members chosen every second year by the people of the several states, and the electors in each state shall have the qualifications requisite for electors of the most numerous branch of the state legislature.

No person shall be a representative who shall not have attained to the age of twenty-five years, and been seven years a citizen of the United States, and who shall not, when elected, be an inhabitant of that state in which he shall be chosen.

Representatives and direct taxes shall be apportioned among the several states which may be included within this Union, according to their respective numbers, which shall be determined by adding to the whole number of free persons, (including those bound to service for a term of years, and excluding Indians not taxed,) three-fifths of all other persons. The actual enumeration shall be made within three years after the first meeting of the Congress of the United States, and within every subsequent term of ten years, in such manner as they shall by law direct. The number of representatives shall not exceed one for every forty thousand, but each state shall have at least one representative: and until such enumeration shall be made, the state of New-Hampshire shall be entitled to chuse three, Massachusetts eight, Rhode-Island and Providence Plantations one, Connecticut five, New-York six, New-Jersey four, Pennsylvania eight, Delaware one, Maryland six, Virginia ten, North-Carolina five, South-Carolina five, and Georgia three.

When vacancies happen in the representation from any state, the Executive authority thereof shall issue writs of election to fill such vacancies.

The House of Representatives shall choose their Speaker and other officers; and shall have the sole power of impeachment.

Sect. 3. The Senate of the United States shall be composed of two senators from each state, chosen by the legislature thereof, for six years: and each senator shall have one vote.

Immediately after they shall be assembled in consequence of the first election, they shall be divided as equally as may be into three classes. The seats of the senators of the first class shall be vacated at the expiration of the second year, of the second class at the expiration of the fourth year, and of the third class at the expiration of the sixth year, so that one-third may be chosen every second year: and if vacancies happen by resignation, or otherwise, during the recess of the Legislature of any state, the Executive thereof may make temporary appointments until the next meeting of the Legislature, *which shall then fill such vacancies.*

No person shall be a senator who shall not have attained to the age of thirty years, and been nine years a citizen of the United States, and who shall not, when elected, be an inhabitant of that state for which he shall be chosen.

The Vice-President of the United States shall be, President of the senate, but shall have no vote, unless they be equally divided.

The Senate shall choose their other officers, and also a President pro tempore, in the absence of the Vice-President, or when he shall exercise the office of President of the United States.

The Senate shall have the sole power to try all impeachments. When sitting for that purpose, they shall be on oath. When the President of the United States is tried, the Chief Justice shall preside: And no person shall be convicted without the concurrence of two-thirds of the members present.

Judgment in cases of impeachment shall not extend further than to removal from office, and disqualification to hold and enjoy any office of honor, trust or profit under the United States: but the party convicted shall nevertheless be liable and subject to indictment, trial, judgment and punishment, according to law.

Sect. 4. The times, places and manner of holding elections for senators and representatives, shall be prescribed in each state by the legislature thereof: but the Congress may at any time by law make or alter such regulations, *except as to the places of chusing senators.*

The Congress shall assemble at least once in every year, and such meeting shall be on the first Monday in December, unless they shall by law appoint a different day.

Sect. 5. Each house shall be the judge of the elections, returns and qualifications of its own members, and a majority of each shall constitute a quorum to do business: but a smaller number may adjourn from day to day, and may be authorised to compel the attendance of absent members, in such manner, and under such penalties as each house may provide.

Each house may determine the rules of its proceedings, punish its members for disorderly behaviour, and, with the concurrence of two-thirds, expel a member.

Each house shall keep a journal of its proceedings, and from time to time publish the same, excepting such parts as may in their judgment require secrecy; and the yeas and nays of the members of either house on any question shall, at the desire of one-fifth of those present, be entered on the journal.

Neither house, during the session of Congress, shall, without the consent of the other, adjourn for more than three days, nor to any other place than that in which the two houses shall be sitting.

Sect. 6. The senators and representatives shall receive a compensation for their services, to be ascertained by law, and paid out of the treasury of the United States. They shall in all cases, except treason, felony and breach of the peace, be privileged from arrest during their attendance at the session of their respective houses, and in going to and returning from the same; and for any speech or debate in either house, they shall not be questioned in any other place.

No senator or representative shall, during the time for which he was elected, be appointed to any civil office under the authority of the United States, which shall have been created, or the emoluments

THE CONSTITUTION
Made Easy

A Tea Partier's Guide

MICHAEL HOLLER

FOREWORD BY FORMER ATTORNEY
GENERAL EDWIN MEESE III

STERLING
New York

STERLING
New York

An Imprint of Sterling Publishing
387 Park Avenue South
New York, NY 10016

ISBN 978-1-4027-9832-0 (hardcover)
ISBN 978-1-4027-8931-1 (ebook)

Distributed in Canada by Sterling Publishing
c/o Canadian Manda Group, 165 Dufferin Street
Toronto, Ontario, Canada M6K 3H6
Distributed in the United Kingdom by GMC Distribution Services
Castle Place, 166 High Street, Lewes, East Sussex, England BN7 1XU
Distributed in Australia by Capricorn Link (Australia) Pty. Ltd.
P.O. Box 704, Windsor, NSW 2756, Australia

FRONTISPIECE: Text of the Constitution as ratified by the Constitutional Convention on September 17,
1787. Printed in Providence, Rhode Island, by John Carter in 1787. Courtesy of the Manuscript
Division, Library of Congress, Const Conv no. 8.
Paper background: © Shutterstock/gillmar

Text of Constitution is from: http://www.archives.gov/exhibits/charters/constitution_transcript.html
*Preamble and Text of Amendments 1–10 is from: http://www.archives.gov/exhibits/charters/bill_of_rights_*
transcript.html
*Text of Amendments 11–27 is from: http://www.archives.gov/exhibits/charters/constitution_*
amendments_11-27.html -- Retrieved August 3, 2011

For information about custom editions, special sales, and premium and corporate purchases, please
contact Sterling Special Sales at 800-805-5489 or specialsales@sterlingpublishing.com.

Manufactured in the United States of America

2 4 6 8 10 9 7 5 3 1

www.sterlingpublishing.com

To all "Oath Keepers" everywhere.

You took the time to read and understand the Constitution.

You swore to defend the Constitution.

Not the country, not the government,
but the *Constitution* of the United States.

Against all enemies, foreign and domestic.

You took the oath. You meant it. Here's to you!

OATH OF OFFICE

"I, _____, do solemnly swear (or affirm) that I will support and defend the Constitution of the United States against all enemies, foreign and domestic; that I will bear true faith and allegiance to the same; that I take this obligation freely, without any mental reservation or purpose of evasion; and that I will well and faithfully discharge the duties of the office on which I am about to enter. So help me God."*

5 U.S.C. 3331

*This is the oath of office required for all members of Congress, and all Federal civil servants since 1884. See Recommended Resources for links to various incarnations of this constitutional-based oath for presidents, judges, and military officers.

CONTENTS

FOREWORD

On the Fourth of July, 1776, the brave signers of the Declaration of Independence pledged their lives, their fortunes, and their sacred honor to support this historic document—and thus a new nation was born. The thirteen colonies, previously belonging to the British Crown, were now free and independent states, able to do all "acts and things which independent [countries] may of right do." It was soon evident, however, that the new nation lacked an effective national government to carry out the responsibilities of defense, diplomatic relationships, and facilitating commerce among the states. For that reason, representatives of the states gathered in Philadelphia in 1787 and drafted a document unique in world history: a *written* constitution.

The Constitution of the United States has been the longest enduring governing document, which establishes the structure of a national government and specifies the principles for its operation. That Constitution is as relevant and important today as it was when ratified by the original states in 1788.

F. A. Hayek stated in *The Constitution of Liberty* (1960), "If old truths are to retain their hold on men's minds, they must be restated in the language and concepts of successive generations." That is why Mike Holler has written *The Constitution Made Easy*: to explain our governing charter in modern language for today's citizens and students. This book does for the common man and woman what extensive commentaries on the Constitution have done for lawyers and serious students of history.

The Founders of our country believed that the Constitution belongs to the teacher and the mechanic as much as to the lawyer and the judge. This book will be a benefit to anyone who has read the Constitution many times, as well as to the person reading it for the first time.

In the Introduction, Mike Holler helps the reader appreciate what the Constitution *is*, before trying to understand what the Constitution *says*. He describes those who seek to distort the Constitution through a theory they call "the living Constitution," and explains the flawed thinking that such a theory represents. He points out that no other legal agreement, certainly one as important as the Constitution, is regarded as changed in its essential meaning as time or technology advance. Thus, it would be singularly destructive to distort the Constitution in this way. Mike explains in simple terms how to regard "original intent" by understanding the history and culture of the time in which the Constitution was drafted and why this "natural" understanding is the only reasonable or consistent way to interpret it.

The Constitution Made Easy guides the reader in a most effective way. The main section is a side-by-side comparison of the original Constitution, with a modern-English, easy-reading version. This is a tool that I recommend for every citizen, regardless of their previous experience and understanding. The modern version can be read in less than half an hour, and the original is always directly opposite for comparison. It is an excellent resource for citizens, students, educators, and elected officials to get their minds around the fundamental concepts, as well as many of the details of governance as expressed by our Founders. Mike has traveled the country teaching the simple precepts of our Founders to the present generation. Our Founders respected life, liberty, and property. They considered self-reliance to be an inherent part of liberty, along with the risks that it entails. After the Revolution, they re-created the "general government" that they had formed during the Revolution, but still intended this "more perfect union" to exist for the benefit of the member States. This new Constitution still limited the general government to enumerated powers; it still respected State sovereignty and protected individual liberty.

Mike believes, as I do, that many of the problems that plague our country today have been caused or made worse by departing from the Constitution, and any effective remedy requires that we return to it. The times and technologies always change, but the principles of governance do not. Either men and women will be free to chart their own courses and accept responsibilities for their decisions, or rulers will make their life choices for them. As Mark Levin has described these choices, they are *liberty* or *tyranny*.

The folks at Tea Party Express call Mike "Mister Constitution" because the Constitution is his single point of reference concerning all matters political. He is an *originalist*, or, as he says, a *naturalist*, who has used his education in translating eighteenth-century language to create a version of the Constitution that is faithful to the original, and yet understandable by nearly any modern reader who will make a modest effort.

I urge *you* to make that effort. The freedom of America, the freedoms of your children, and the rest of the children in the world may depend on whether we Americans, reading these words today, adhere to the principles of freedom the Constitution prescribes. Then, we must compel our government officials to return to the constitutional fidelity required by their oaths of office, or elect new officials who will. As my old boss Ronald Reagan was fond of saying:

> Freedom is never more than one generation away from extinction. We didn't pass it to our children in the bloodstream. It must be fought for, protected, and handed on for them to do the same, or one day we will spend our sunset years telling our children and our children's children what it was once like in the United States where men were free.

Edwin Meese III
Attorney General of the United States (1985–88)
McLean, Virginia
November 28, 2011

GUIDE TO UNDERSTANDING AND ENJOYING THIS BOOK

For most people, reading the United States Constitution is difficult, and no wonder—it was written in "legalese," and most of it is more than two hundred years old. But now, *The Constitution Made Easy* not only offers a modernized version for easier reading; it actually makes the meaning of the original seem to jump off the page.

Great effort was made to preserve the original meaning and intent of the Founding Fathers in this modern English version; and because the original text is displayed side-by-side with the modern text for comparison, *The Constitution Made Easy* becomes a reference you can trust. The Constitution and all the Amendments in this volume were carefully copied from the version maintained by the United States Government at the National Archives. The reader is invited to visit the Archives at: www.archives.gov/exhibits.

How to Use *The Constitution Made Easy*

Here are a few details and some unique features of *The Constitution Made Easy* that will make your reading more enjoyable and understandable.

The original Constitution will *always* be on the left-hand page and the modern English version will *always* be on the right. The two versions look very different from each other and are also easily identified by the phrases at the bottom of each page: "U.S. Constitution" on the left-hand pages and "The Constitution Made Easy" on the right-hand pages.

Now, some facts about the original: The body of the Constitution has seven large divisions called **Articles**. Each Article discusses a new subject, such as Congress, the President, or the Supreme Court. The divisions within Articles are called **Sections**, and the divisions within Sections are called **Clauses**. Any given Clause is normally referred to by its location, such as in Article I, Section VIII, Clause VII. (This particular Clause concerns the Post Office.) Roman numerals are used in the original.

A modern numbering plan was adopted in the modern version, so that same Clause would be referred to as Article 1, Section 8, Clause 7. A *shorthand* way of referring to it would be simply **1.8.7**. At the end of the Articles are the signatures of the State delegates. When the Constitution was first approved (ratified) this is all there was.

Then there are twenty-seven **Amendments**, also known as **Articles of Amendment**, that come after these first seven Articles. Like the seven original Articles, Articles of Amendment may be divided into Sections, and several of them have been. In the modern version, one of these Sections (Amendment 20, Section 3) has even been divided into two Clauses.

Until now, one of the great barriers to understanding the Constitution was that an Amendment sometimes modified just a few words, and sometimes it completely replaced (or *superseded*) one or more full Clauses. In the National Archives version, the language that has been replaced or modified is <u>underlined</u>, and then the Amendment that affected it is cited in brackets [like this].

Without a modern version to compare to, readers typically find themselves jumping forward to locate the Amendment, then jumping back to the original, and trying to mentally integrate the effects of the changes. In some cases, this can be so frustrating that even a patient reader may decide to put the Constitution down "for now anyway" (and sometimes does not return to it).

The Constitution Made Easy does this work for you. The

contemporary "translation" and explanation of the effects of each Amendment are included *right in the text* of the modern English version. If the effect was modest, only the pertinent words or phrases will be added or replaced. If the effect was substantial (as you will see in Article 2, Section 1), then whole Amendments may be included in the modern version to provide greater clarity.

In these instances there will be more Clauses in the modern version than in the original. This also creates "gaps," or blank lines, in a few places in the original. To help keep it clear, the original will have [bracketed] information referring to the Amendment that replaced the original wording, and the modern version will likewise refer to it, either in [brackets] or in an endnote. There should never be any real need to flash back and forth between the original and the Amendments in order to understand the current meaning.

It is easy to tell where paragraphs in the original begin and end, even if there is "white space" in the middle. If any line begins at the left margin, this indicates a new paragraph in the original. If it is indented, it is a continuation of the paragraph above it.

The full texts of all the Amendments are still included after the "amended" body of the Constitution, so some of the language will be seen for a second time. This will be especially noticeable in the 12th, 20th, and 25th Amendments, which greatly affected Article 2, Section 1. Also noteworthy is Amendment 17, which affected the election of Senators (Article 1, Section 3).

There is also an endnotes section that provides even more details, definitions, and explanations.

One more note about the shorthand numbering system. When a specific item of text in the body of the Constitution or in an Amendment is being referred to, the letter *C* added in front of the numbers indicates the body of the Constitution, and the letter *A* indicates an Amendment.

So for example, **C:1.8.7** indicates the Constitution: Article 1, Section 8, Clause 7; while Amendment 20, Section 3, Clause 2 would be written **A:20.3.2**. These are in **bold type** for ease of reference.

This translation, *The Constitution Made Easy*, strives to convey the original intent of the Founders in modern language that retains (nearly) the exact same meaning, but in words that flow more naturally for twenty-first-century readers. The goal is to communicate original intent, not modern usage; to make it understandable, not necessarily palatable. It is not a living translation, but a literal one. At times, even a phrase or capitalization that would seem unusual today is retained if there was a meaning intended that might otherwise be lost or lessened.

As a final thought, *The Constitution Made Easy* is much easier to understand than the original, but is not intended to replace it for serious study. Almost anyone can read this modern version (the odd-numbered pages) in under thirty minutes, and should be able to grasp the essential propositions and themes underlying the foundational document of our republic. It is hoped that this will then inspire the reader to read and study the original, perhaps using the modern version and endnotes as tools.

The Constitution is "the supreme law of the land." Virtually every elected and public official in America takes an oath to uphold it. The President promises to "preserve, protect, and defend" it. The Branches of U.S. Government chart (see page 100) shows Congress, the President, and the Supreme Court *underneath* the Constitution.

The Constitution has been called the greatest governing document ever written. Understanding it is worth the effort, and now easier than ever before. Enjoy!

INTRODUCTION
An Honest Understanding of the United States Constitution

What damned error, but some sober brow
Will bless it, and approve it with a text,
Hiding the grossness with fair ornament?

—WILLIAM SHAKESPEARE, *MERCHANT OF VENICE*,
ACT III, SCENE 2

There are two very different methods of interpreting the Constitution; only one of them can be right, and the future of the free world may hang in the balance. The two techniques are not driven by intellectual disagreements about what the document says, but by political convictions about the proper role of Government.

Original versus Living Document

The first method uses the same *objective* approach that is applied to most written works, and considers the task from the perspective of history and the meaningful use of language. The goal is to discover the meaning that the writers intended, without regard to the consequences of that discovery. It takes into consideration the authorship, the occasion on which the author(s) wrote the document, the intended audience, the literary genre, and the design of the document itself. The people who approach the Constitution this way are often referred to as *originalists*.

One could just as accurately refer to them as *naturalists*: people who simply want to appreciate the meaning of the literature they read and study in the same way as the people who wrote and read that literature, at the time and place in which they lived—meaning that sprang naturally from the time and place in which the text was written. This is the method used by honest scholars in their approach to every other written work by writers from Cicero to Solzhenitsyn. While these originalists all have personal prejudices and political views that will unavoidably have some effect on their analysis, at least they endeavor to approach the text with objectivity, they build consensus on most major questions, and they agree on the basis for further debate. Adherents to originalism believe the meaning of the Constitution can only be changed by Amendment, not by legislation, culture, or even war. They regard it as the supreme law of the land and agree that Governments in every branch, at every level, are to be bound by it.

The second method can only be called a *magical method*. It permits the Constitution to mean whatever the interpreter wants or needs it to mean at a given moment. This *subjective* or *supernatural* approach is often pursued by recognized scholars with impressive credentials who would never admit to practicing magic. But they know that they are working toward a predetermined goal, rather than intending to draw out the original meaning. They often say nice things about the Constitution: that it is a living document, a truly amazing work, a wise and wonderful creation, and the like. But their flowery words are designed to mask their political objective—the goal of concentrating great power, or even absolute power, in a central Government. Truth be known, they usually believe that the Constitution should be a dead document, and they wish to kill it. Their Constitution changes a little or a lot with every election and Supreme Court nomination.

These are bold claims, but claims borne out by the facts. Their underlying political beliefs drive these bright men and women to their nonsensical conclusions. Simply put, the Constitution, taken at face value, places limits on what the Federal Government may do, and these people do not want our Federal Government to be limited by those boundaries. To that end, they employ a subjective method to arrive at the conclusion that the Government may do, and even should do, whatever it is that it wants to do at the moment. This is precisely what they mean when they refer to it as a "living document." Their nice words usually go something like this: "It is living in the sense that it can meet the needs of a changing society and permit Government the latitude it needs in order to remain relevant." But this is not very different from admitting that "The Constitution says what we *want* it to say, because that is what we *need* it to say, so that we are able to *do* what we plan to *do*."

To be fair, some people who hold the liberal-progressive–living-document view truly believe that a Government unlimited by anything except the will of the Governors, elected by the will of the people, is the best kind of Government there is. They believe that elected leaders can do much good for their country and all of humankind if they are not bound by a legal document that constrains them. Some of them may be well-intentioned, but their belief is belied by history. There is not an example in all of recorded history where an unlimited Government produced the utopia they seek. Winston Churchill said it like this in 1948:

> Socialism is a philosophy of failure, the creed of ignorance, and the gospel of envy.[1]

What the historical examples do show are societies with more or less equal distributions of misery and poverty; I say more or less because the economic status of the peasant class always rises or falls a few degrees within the confines of poverty, but the ruling class (be they members of Politburos or pharaonic dynasties) is always excluded from the misery their tyranny creates. Despots like Saddam Hussein enjoyed the kind of wealth and luxury that Wall Street tycoons might envy. Kim Jong-un appears to be about the only portly man in North Korea, where an estimated two million people starved to death after the collapse of the Soviet Union.

And the worst forms of despotism have been bloodbaths. Some statisticians estimate that, in the twentieth century, Governments murdered more than twice as many civilians as were killed in all the international and domestic wars combined.

And, to be fair to originalists, they do not believe that the Constitution is unchangeable; only that it ought to be binding until changed by the Amendment process. As George Washington said in his 1796 presidential Farewell Address:

> But the Constitution which at any time exists, till changed by an explicit and authentic act of the whole people, is sacredly obligatory upon all. The very idea of the power and the right of the people to establish government presupposes the duty of every individual to obey the established government.[2]

The magical, living-document view has been adhered to by many, if not most, of all Federal elected and appointed officials for almost a hundred years, at least since the Administration of Woodrow Wilson, and the damage done has been staggering. Today, the Federal Government does almost anything it pleases. Elected officials buy votes from special-interest groups, and coalitions of special-interest groups. The officials do things for these groups and promise to do more, with the twin objectives of remaining in power and increasing their power. Welfare is no longer just for the poor, but also for the very rich, and Government buys votes from both. Government is no longer content to redistribute wealth between the poor and the middle class; it now picks winners and losers on Wall Street and distorts the free market with tax credits and subsidies. Congresses and Presidents alternately take the side of labor or management, border patrol or illegal immigrants—whichever seems more advantageous to the party in power at the moment. And, when necessary, they cite a provision in the Constitution as cover. George Orwell's words are prescient: "[P]olitical speech and writing are largely the defense of the indefensible."³

But does the Constitution permit these actions that coincidentally happen to be politically expedient? Or is it being exploited for personal ambition and political gain? If the originalists are right, the second scenario is usually the case. And in abusing the original meaning of the Constitution, our elected officials have spent the nation into a debt and deficit crisis. When Ronald Reagan was elected in 1980, he said Government "is too big and spends too much." Today we spend *six times* as much as in 1980. Yet we are often told that every program is "absolutely essential" (and also running at peak efficiency). It seems that not one program can ever be cut 1 percent, which makes another of Reagan's witticisms ring true: "[G]overnments' programs, once launched, never disappear. Actually, a government bureau is the nearest thing to eternal life we'll ever see on this earth."⁴ At this writing, every baby born in the United States today inherits about $50,000 in Government debt, with more on the way. Every "tax-paying taxpayer" owes five times that amount (since nearly half the people counted by the Government as "taxpayers" actually pay no tax at all). This debt does not include staggering shortfalls projected in entitlement spending on Social Security and Medicare. Economist Paul Prentice sums up the debt accumulation and market interference like this: "If Capitalism ever does completely drown, it will be because of the Government's best efforts to pull it down."[5] Our nation is in deep economic trouble. Elected officials say and do things that the average person knows will only make things worse. Howard Kaloogian of Tea Party Express keeps the message simple: "You can't spend your way out of a deficit, and you cannot borrow your way out of debt."[6] He advises that the elected officials who have dug us into this hole should "quit digging." Yet with a national debt equal to the nation's total production, they are still spending borrowed money by the trillions and calling it "stimulus." It has been many years since anyone in leadership in either party has even *proposed* to balance the Federal budget. Not even the Republicans' plan balances the Federal budget, not even ten years from now.

Americans of every political stripe are becoming concerned about a rogue Government and about spending that is unsustainable—hence, the rise of the so-called "Tea Party." I have spoken and held book signings at over two hundred Tea Parties or similar events, meeting thousands of Tea Partiers one-on-one, and know the movement well. The most common force that impels people to attend their first Tea Party is a gut feeling that something is terribly wrong with our Government. Not one person I have met has ever expressed concern to me that we had elected a black President. Some of them even voted for Obama, sometimes in part because he is African-American, but regretted it later because of his actions. These same "racists" would gladly vote for a different black President who shared their concerns.

The Tea Party movement has never been about race or even about political parties, cries heard in the mainstream media notwithstanding. As Tea Partiers became educated, they realized that these problems of enormous debt and invasive "command and control" Government had been building for decades, and that the "progressives" in both major parties share the responsibility for a Government gone wild. Most of them did not understand the Constitution when they first "got up off the sofa," but many proved to be quick studies. The Tea Party is not a political party, has no one leader, and the "members" disagree on at least as many issues as they agree. But this much seems clear to nearly all of them: the wisdom of our Founders has been ignored for a very long time, and we are reaping the whirlwind. The Constitution set boundaries on Government, and those boundaries have been obliterated. James Madison warned us, "Wherever there is power and interest to do wrong, wrong will generally be done." Thomas Jefferson used even more specific language (**boldface** mine):

> Free government is founded in jealousy, and not in confidence; it is jealousy and not confidence which prescribes **limited constitutions, to bind** down those we are obliged to trust with power. . . . In questions of power, then, let no more be heard of confidence in men, but **bind him down from mischief by the chains of the Constitution.**[7]

The purpose of our Constitution is to bind power and unleash liberty. The purpose of Statists (those who advocate highly centralized governments, by whatever name) is to unleash power and bind liberty. Constitutions only get in the Statists' way, and they will use any means necessary to abrogate them. They will ignore, infringe, abridge, usurp, negotiate, barter, banter, bargain, torture, and twist the language and the public sentiment to achieve their ends. They will patiently replace principle with practice; replace statute with precedent; and go over, under, around, or through the barriers that keep them from absolute power.

In Oliver Stone's 2010 film *Wall Street: Money Never Sleeps*, Shia LaBeouf, who plays a stockbroker, asks Josh Brolin, who portrays a Wall Street banker, "I find that everybody has a number [meaning how much wealth he would need to amass before he would be satisfied], and it's usually an exact number, so what is yours?" Brolin gives the same answer that Statists give when asked how much more power they need. He says simply, and dramatically, "More." Political ambition and the lust for power are often just greater forms of greed.

According to our Founders, power lust is part of human nature. Madison said, "[P]ower, lodged as it must be in human hands will ever be liable to abuse."[8] Tyrants like Mao and Stalin wanted power and knew the bloodshed needed to acquire it would be horrendous. But some kinder and gentler Statists truly believe that only Government can solve the ills that societies face. They may even believe that just a little more will be enough. Just a little more money, and a little more control—that's all they might think they need. But this "progress," as envisioned by "progressives," is always in one direction, and that direction is inexorably toward absolute despotism. At this point in American history, the Constitution still remains an obstacle, but one they have violated routinely and with impunity for a very long time. Only a sustained revival of the American spirit and a vigorous assertion of a literal reading of the Constitution can save it, and what was once America, from oblivion. It must be firmly established and forcefully defended that the Constitution is supreme not only in the powers it grants, but in the bright white boundaries around those powers.

What the Constitution Is

Before we have a chance at agreeing on what the Constitution *says*, we must have clarity on what it *is*. In the fewest possible words, the Constitution is a contract between the States, whereby they (the States) created a general Government for their benefit. It granted "powers" to this new general Government to do certain things for the States that the States could not reasonably or feasibly do for themselves. Some examples are maintaining a single post office, having one standard for weights and measurements, coining money, granting patents and copyrights, and maintaining a single Navy. Then it strictly limited the new Government to the powers that were granted by the contract, in language that was intended to be unambiguous and unmistakable.

It is impossible to imagine that the Founders intended anything else. They had just led their people in a bloody revolution and secured independence for each of their colonies. In the words of the Declaration of Independence, they had now become "Free and Independent States" (plural). They had taken their places among the nations of the world. No sane student of history would even venture to suggest that these freedom fighters would immediately surrender their whole independence to a new Government of any sort whatever; as opposed to "original intent," this would have to be called "impossible intent." None of the leaders of these newly freed States would have surrendered their sovereignty, nor would their constituents have permitted it.

The late colonies had but recently become compactly organized, self-governing States, and were standing somewhat stiffly apart, a group of consequential sovereignties, jealous to maintain their blood-bought prerogatives, and quick to distrust any power set above them, or arrogating to itself the control of their restive wills. It was not to be expected that the sturdy, self-reliant, masterful men who had won independence for their native colonies, by passing through the flames of battle, and through the equally fierce fires of bereavement and financial ruin, would readily transfer their affection and allegiance from the new-made States, which were their homes, to the federal government, which was to be a mere artificial creation, and which could be to no man as his home government.

—Woodrow Wilson, *Congressional Government: A Study in American Politics*, 1885[9]

Instead, they decided to simply improve upon the Confederation that had allowed them to work together and fight as one to win their independence. A few years after the Treaty of Paris, they drafted and ratified the United States Constitution, forging "a more perfect Union."

Their original intent is clear from the two kinds of historical evidence available to us. The first is the "internal" evidence: what is found inside the document itself, including the words and phrases the Framers chose, the order in which they appear, and the outline of the document. The second source is the "external" evidence. This evidence includes the underlying documents that predate the drafting of the Constitution, the contemporary documents written during the time of the Constitutional Convention and the State ratifying conventions, and the "Founding Era" documents that include early legislation and opinions of the Founders in the years shortly after ratification.

Which brings us back to the central purpose of our Constitution—or any constitution, for that matter. The only reason to have a written constitution is to limit Government, because a Government can be the friend or the enemy of rights and freedom. The Declaration of Independence famously says "that all men are created equal, that they are endowed by their Creator with certain unalienable Rights, that among these are Life, Liberty and the pursuit of Happiness." But it goes on to tell us that the reason to have Government is "to secure these rights." Then it warns us that Government can be "destructive" to the very purpose for which it was created. Government is necessary; but it is also dangerous. It can secure our rights, or strip them from us, and so the need for boundaries—a Constitution.

Hypothetically, it would be a simple matter for a group of people to choose how they would be ruled and go about being ruled. They could choose to be ruled by a President, a dictator, or a Governor; or a Congress, a Parliament, or a Politburo. They would simply choose their rulers and be done with it. There would be no limits on how long rulers and other officials would serve or what edicts they could enforce. Or perhaps they would choose a direct democracy where everyone votes on everything. But unless they have a written agreement about who is allowed to participate, what limits they will have, and how minority interests will be protected, even a direct democracy of this sort would quickly result in mob rule.

The reason we have written constitutions is so that Government officials will be chosen in a certain way, for a certain period of time, and have specific responsibilities and clear limits on their powers. Then if the constitution is well-written and faithfully executed and enforced, it will not matter very much how many people are elected or appointed, or how old they must be in order to serve. Even the great question of whether there is to be one branch of Government, or three, is less important than having well-defined duties and boundaries those in power.

The United States Constitution was drafted by men who were familiar with world history and human nature, subjects seldom faced squarely today. They knew that all Governments tended toward tyranny and they were determined to constitute the sort of Government that would have many safeguards against such abuse. Thomas Jefferson wrote, "The natural progress of things is for liberty to yeild [sic], and government to gain ground."[10] Ronald Reagan may have been paraphrasing Jefferson when he said, "Remember that every government service . . . is paid for in the loss of personal freedom."[11]

Limited Government

If the federal government should overpass the just bounds of its authority and make a tyrannical use of its powers, the people, whose creature it is, must appeal to the standard they have formed, and take such measures to redress the injury done to the Constitution as the exigency may suggest and prudence justify.

—ALEXANDER HAMILTON, "FEDERALIST NO. 33,"
DECEMBER 26, 1787[12]

We earlier defined the Constitution as "a contract between the States, whereby they [the States] created a general Government for their benefit." If we accept that definition, it would be fair to ask, "How do we know that they intended for this Government to be limited, and where would the limits be?" The answer is found in hundreds of places; but the best place to begin is in the first five words of the first Article of the Constitution itself.

"All legislative Powers herein granted," means all powers to write laws are granted *in here*. The powers that are about to be listed will be entrusted to Congress. If the Framers had meant to say, "all Powers whatsoever," they would have said that, and that was certainly an option discussed at the Convention. The fact that it was considered and rejected is also worth noting, but the result of the deliberation of the delegates was to limit the powers to the ones listed.

And we should pause here to ask: What exactly are these "powers" anyway? "Powers" are authority that has been delegated, and in our Founders' view, the final authorities are "We, the People." According to them, we are given "rights" by our Creator that can never be removed from our personality. Our ability to fully exercise and enjoy our rights can be diminished or even denied, but never alienated from the essence of who we are as human beings, created in the image of God. When we delegate some of our authority to a Government, that is called a power, and our Founders were scrupulous to use the terms that way.[13] We should never question whether any Government agency has the "right" to do a certain thing; it does not. It may or may not have the power to do it, and if it does, the power may or may not be properly conferred. Power taken without being properly granted is referred to by our Founders as being "usurped" or arrogated.

At the Founding, we, the people (or rather, "they, the people"), in every State had already delegated some of their authority to their State Government. The Constitution created a general Government of the States, and "they, the States," in turn, delegated some of their authority to the new general Government. The second way we would discover that powers were to be limited is that they were written out—(like the rest of the Constitution) in longhand—in Article 1, Section 8. There were many lists made, voted down in whole or in part, tossed aside, and rewritten. Why would the Founders have bothered to write the lists out, debate them, and write them out again if they meant to include powers not listed? They would not have! Yet a document hangs right in Independence Hall in Philadelphia, written by modern interpreters, which says there are also "implied powers" in the Constitution. Nothing could be further from the intent of the Founders. We will have more to say about this doctrine of implied powers shortly.

The third place we could look inside the Constitution is the last power in Article 1, Section 8 **(C:1.8)**. It says Congress shall have Power

> To make all Laws which shall be necessary and proper for carrying into Execution the foregoing Powers, and all other Powers vested by this Constitution in the Government of the United States, or in any Department or Officer thereof.

This paragraph will be considered at greater length a little later, because it is one of the three big "loopholes" that progressives have used to find new power (even though its purpose is quite the opposite). For now, we simply note that lawmaking is limited to the powers just listed ("foregoing") and other powers granted ("vested") elsewhere in this same Constitution.

A fourth piece of evidence that the powers of the new general Government were to be limited is found in the "Supremacy Clause" (the second paragraph of Article 6, **C:6.2**):

> This Constitution, and the Laws of the United States which shall be made in Pursuance thereof; and all Treaties made, or which shall be made, under the Authority of the United States, shall be the supreme Law of the Land; and the Judges in every State shall be bound thereby, any Thing in the Constitution or Laws of any State to the Contrary notwithstanding.

For now we can simply note that for "Laws of the United States" to be considered "supreme," they are to be made pursuant to the Constitution; they are to conform with it, and properly derive their authority from it.

Finally, the 10th Amendment is deliberately redundant. It acts as a "backstop" in case the concept of enumerated powers got lost or ignored:

> The powers not delegated to the United States by the Constitution, nor prohibited by it to the States, are reserved to the States respectively, or to the people.

Read without the subordinate clause in the middle, it says:

> The powers not delegated to the United States by the Constitution . . . are reserved to the States respectively.

So if a power is not granted to the Federal Government by this Constitution, then it is retained by the States. That is, unless the Constitution also prohibits the States from having a certain power, in which case it remains with the ultimate source of sovereignty—the people. External sources confirm this. The Articles of Confederation, which were our first "Constitution," listed most of the same powers of Congress, but were explicitly clear when they said:

> Each state retains its sovereignty, freedom, and independence, and
> every power, jurisdiction, and right, which is not by this Confederation
> expressly delegated to the United States, in Congress assembled.

The entire deliberation of the Constitutional Convention concerned what powers the new Government should have. But even more significantly, the ratification by the States was only made possible by the plain language of the Constitution and the many representations made by the Federalists (supporters of Constitutional ratification) that there was no intent to go further, and that adequate safeguards were in place to prevent it. A person taking the time to read the Federalist Papers would reasonably conclude that they are hundreds of pages of promises to limit the new general Government to a judicious exercise of only the specific powers granted. Sadly, these writers (James Madison, Alexander Hamilton, and John Jay) could only promise what they would do in their own lifetimes, and trust that the language and other safeguards they had installed would be sufficient thereafter. In "Federalist No. 45," James Madison writes (**boldface** mine):

> The powers delegated by the proposed Constitution to the federal
> government, are **few and defined**. Those which are to remain in the
> State governments are **numerous and indefinite**. The former will be
> exercised principally on external objects, as war, peace, negotiation, and

foreign commerce; with which last the power of taxation will, for the most part, be connected. The powers reserved to the several States will extend to all the objects which, in the ordinary course of affairs, concern the lives, liberties, and properties of the people, and the internal order, improvement, and prosperity of the State.[14]

The Loopholes

The obstacles to usurpation and the facilities of resistance increase with the increased extent of the state, provided the citizens understand their rights and are disposed to defend them.

—Alexander Hamilton, "Federalist No. 28," December 26, 1787[15]

People who are not well acquainted with American history and the Constitution deserve to know how it got this way. If the Constitution is a limiting document, how did we end up with a nearly unlimited Government? The answer lies in the human heart, and in the loopholes.

For about a generation after the Founding, the Constitution was usually honored. Certainly there were instances where a Congress, a President, or a Court overstepped their bounds. But by today's standards, the infringements were generally minor, and the greater ones (such as the Sedition Acts of 1798) were either rebuffed or at least hotly contested at the time. In most instances, the discussions on both sides of these contests showed a high regard for the Constitution. As Woodrow Wilson wrote in his famous book, *Congressional Government*:

> The very men who had resisted with might and main the adoption of the Constitution became, under the new division of parties, its champions, as sticklers for a strict, a rigid, and a literal construction. They

were consistent enough in this, because it was quite natural that their one-time fear of a strong central government should pass into a dread of the still further expansion of the power of that government, by a too loose construction of its charter.[16]

Over time, efforts were made to justify the actions of a Congress or a President using "loopholes," or, as they have been so subtly recast, "implied powers," a doctrine Woodrow Wilson called "both facile and irresistible." He went on to describe some of the consequences of that doctrine, which he himself deemed necessary and constitutional:

> Of course every new province into which Congress has been allured by the principle of implied powers has required for its administration a greater or less enlargement of the national civil service, which now, through its hundred thousand officers, carries into every community of the land a sense of federal power, as the power of powers, and fixes the federal authority, as it were, in the very habits of society.[17]

The "implied powers" that have been most commonly abused over the years fall under the categories of "General Welfare," "Interstate Commerce," and "Necessary and Proper."

We will see in the next few pages how the context and meaning of the original words were distorted to permit the latitude of powers assumed by the Federal Government. But a larger question deserves to be asked: Why would people entrusted with power, and who took an oath to remain inside the boundaries of the Constitution, want so very badly to find a way around those boundaries?

The oath of office that all members of Congress have taken since 1884 opens with, "I, _____, do solemnly swear (or affirm) that I will support and defend the Constitution of the United States against all enemies, foreign and domestic." It does not say, "I will do my best to expand my powers beyond the ones granted," and it makes one contemplate at what point the deliberate torturing of the agreement these people swear to defend makes them a domestic enemy of it.

The oath goes on to say, "I will bear true faith and allegiance to the same [the Constitution of the United States]." In our day, we cannot help but wonder—who is bearing true faith and allegiance to whom? Are our elected officials bending their wills in order to honor the Constitution, or is the Constitution being bent to the will of our Government?

It continues, "That I take this obligation freely, without any mental reservation or purpose of evasion." How could an oath be any more eloquent or pure? And as if it needed anything to confirm it, the oath finishes with, "So help me God." In case overuse has made the phrase seem trite, we should be reminded that this is a short prayer, "God please help me keep the oath that I just swore." If this "swearing in" is not clear enough to place the oath-taker under the authority of the Constitution, and not the other way around, then God help us all.

It should be evident prima facie that the Constitution delegates a numbered list of powers to the United States, that all other powers are retained by the States or the people, and that the oath of office was required because of the danger of usurpation. Holding an office of power comes as a trust not to abuse that power or overstep the limits of that power; hence, bright white boundaries and a crystal-clear oath. What Woodrow Wilson and others who followed him called "implied powers," our Founders called "abridgement," "encroachment," and "usurpation." On June 6, 1788, James Madison gave a speech at the Virginia Convention to ratify the Federal Constitution, where he remarked:

> Since the general civilization of mankind, I believe there are more
> instances of the abridgment of the freedom of the people by gradual
> and silent encroachments of those in power, than by violent and sudden
> usurpations.[18]

Though it should be morally unthinkable to evade the plain meaning of that oath, historically Presidents and Congresses have used certain loopholes to expand their powers, and courts have often been complicit. This would come as no surprise to the Founders, who were clearly concerned about possible usurpations. (The word usurpation is used twenty times in the Federalist Papers alone.) What might surprise them, however, is that we have not boldly asserted and jealously guarded the freedoms paid for by their sacrifice. So that the reader might do so with greater confidence, the three loopholes most commonly employed as devices against the plain meaning of the Constitution will now be examined.

General Welfare

With respect to the words "general welfare," I have always regarded them as qualified by the detail of powers connected with them. To take them in a literal and unlimited sense would be a metamorphosis of the Constitution into a character which there is a host of proofs was not contemplated by its creators.

—JAMES MADISON, LETTER FROM JAMES MADISON TO JAMES ROBERTSON, APRIL 20, 1831[19]

Nothing sounds more agreeable than the idea that Congress should work for our general welfare. Every effort they put forward would be for our good and we would be ungrateful if we did not appreciate their many kindnesses.

Unfortunately, history teaches us that any Government granted the power to provide for *our* welfare actually provides only for *its* own. Our Congress, to the degree that it has arrogated powers to provide for us, has predictably redistributed our wealth according to their whims du jour, and enriched themselves and their friends in the process. As the nineteenth-century British historian and politician Lord Acton observed, "Power tends to corrupt, and absolute power corrupts absolutely."

It will come as a surprise to many readers that the Constitution does not give Congress *any* authority to provide for the welfare of the *people* of the United States. It only gives Congress a short list of powers that fall under the *category* of "general welfare." Further, the welfare spoken of is not the welfare of the people, per se, but the welfare of the States. The relationship between the general Government and the people was, for the most part, an indirect one.

How can we possibly know this? The Supreme Court does not regard it this way. None of us ever learned such things in public school. We can know this for certain from two sources: English grammar and history.

The grammar is straightforward. Article I, Section 8, Clause 1 **(C:1.8.1)** says that Congress will have power to lay and collect various kinds of taxes in order "to pay the debts and provide for the common Defence and general Welfare of the United States."

This sounds pretty broad, and it is. If left there, the powers of Congress would be vague enough that no one would know for certain exactly what was granted, and what, if anything, was forbidden. In fact, Jefferson said that if these were the only words, "It would reduce the whole [Constitution] to a single phrase, that of instituting a Congress with power to do whatever would be good for the United States."[20]

Fortunately, the framers of the Constitution were more specific— much more. As Madison said, these words are "qualified by the detail of powers connected with them." Jefferson added, "Certainly no such universal power was meant to be given them."[21]

The phrases general welfare and common defense are categories. The "detail of powers connected with them [general welfare]" are enumerated as **C:1.8.2–9** and **C:1.8.17**. In the same way, the detail of common defense powers are enumerated as **C:1.8.10–16**.

We also learn from history that general welfare means for the benefit of the States generally, as opposed to something that would favor one State or a group of States. This may be seen most plainly in the Articles of Confederation, Article 3 (**boldface** mine):

> The said **States** hereby severally enter into a firm league of friendship with **each other**, for **their** common defense, the security of **their** liberties, and **their** mutual and **general welfare**, binding **themselves** to assist **each other**, against all force offered to, or attacks made upon **them**, or **any of them**, on account of religion, sovereignty, trade, or any other pretense whatever.

Clearly, general welfare as used in the Articles meant the well-being of the States. Madison makes it clear that this phrase was copied into the Constitution, and retained the same meaning. In the Virginia Resolutions of 1798, he writes that "certain *general phrases* (which having been copied from the very limited grant of powers in the former Articles of Confederation, were the less liable to be misconstrued)."[22] In case there was any doubt as to which general phrases he had in mind, he removed that doubt thirteen months later in the Virginia Report of 1800, "The general phrases here meant must be those of 'providing for the common defence and general welfare.'"[23] Even Jefferson's quote (endnote 20 on opposite page) worries that a single phrase (general welfare) would allow Congress to do whatever it decided was "good for the United States"; not the people, as such.

When one looks at the "detail of powers connected with [general welfare]," it is clear that borrowing money was to be for a purpose that benefited every State. Making trade flow freely, standardizing naturalization and bankruptcy laws, coining money, punishing counterfeiters, running the post office, granting patents and copyrights, and creating a Federal Court system benefited every State. General benefits do not require the precision of equal or pro rata benefits, but must at minimum apply to all States in a general way.

The phrase United States is actually a plural term. Wherever a pronoun is used to refer to them in the Constitution itself, their plural nature becomes absolutely clear. Article 1, Section 9, Clause 8 **(C:1.9.8)** says, "No Title of Nobility shall be granted by the United States: And no Person holding any Office of Profit or Trust under *them* . . . " Article 2, Section 1, Clause 7 **(C:2.1.7)** adds, "The President shall [receive a salary, but] . . . shall not receive within that Period any other Emolument from the United States, or *any of them*." Article 3, Section 3, clause 1 **(C:3.3.1)** adds still further, "Treason against the United States, shall consist only in levying War against *them*, or in adhering to *their* Enemies" (emphasis mine). The Articles of Confederation name each State in the Preamble, then follow immediately with Article I: "The Stile of this Confederacy shall be 'The United States of America.'"

The several States created a Government for themselves that would serve them, not rule over them. They created a Government of the States, by the States, and for the States. This Government was for their benefit, to allow them to do in unison what they could not reasonably or feasibly do separately. They left all matters that were not delegated to the control of the general Government up to the State Governments or the people. They were a union of nation-states, not a melting pot of counties, or a single unit. They had "general [or common] interests" (Articles of Confederation, Article V), and needed a common defense. The two purposes of common defense and general welfare are spelled out in enumerated detail. According to Madison, it is not sufficient for a law to reference one of these categories; it must also be consistent with "the detail of powers connected with them."

Over time, and with complicity from the courts, Congress has done exactly as Jefferson feared; using "a single phrase"—general welfare—to grant itself power to do whatever it thought was good. Jefferson's complaint about this arrangement was that "as they would be the sole judges of the good or evil, it would be also a power to do whatever evil they please."

Interstate Commerce

> *I own myself the friend to a very free*
> *system of commerce, and hold it as a truth,*
> *that commercial shackles are generally unjust,*
> *oppressive and impolitic.*[24]
>
> —JAMES MADISON, "IMPORT DUTIES, HOUSE OF
> REPRESENTATIVES," APRIL 9, 1789

Of the "Big Three" loopholes that Congress has worked on to expand its powers, the "Commerce Clause" has become the favorite. This is not because it actually confers the kind of power Congress wants, but because the courts have gradually opened this door until it invites nearly any legislation that can be imagined. The most expansive example of this to date is the Health Care Reform legislation.

Now this clause is being put to the ultimate test. If the Commerce Clause empowers Congress to force American citizens to purchase something, under any pretext, the coup is complete. There will no longer be anything that our Imperial Congress cannot force us to do or not to do, according to its whims, the whole of the Constitution notwithstanding. This is exactly what Woodrow Wilson meant by the title of his book, *Congressional Government*, where he writes:

All niceties of constitutional restriction and even many broad principles of constitutional limitation have been overridden, and a thoroughly organized system of congressional control set up.[25]

The concepts of limited Federal Government, enumerated powers, State sovereignty, and individual liberty will finally all be finished. The Government will be supreme and we will owe our very existence to its caprice. It may furnish health care, or refuse it. Life and death will be in the hands of a new bureaucracy, created and controlled by Congress. If this is not the definition of Statism, it is certainly slouching toward it.

Absolute control is the ultimate object of our Federal Government,[26] as it has been the goal of every other Government that has ever sat, and the Constitution will no longer stand in the way. We will still have what Wilson called the constitutional "form of government rather in name than in reality." But we will have replaced the substance with nothing but "a scheme of congressional supremacy."[27]

Maybe it is inevitable, but we ought to look at how badly the Commerce Clause has been tortured to set up this endgame. Does this Clause grant anything like the power now being asserted? It does so only if history can be stood on its head, and the English language turned inside out.

The exact wording of Article 1, Section 8, Clause 3 (**C:1.8.3**) is that Congress shall have the power "To regulate Commerce with foreign Nations, and among the several States, and with the Indian Tribes." At the time, the definition of commerce was "trade," and the definition of regulate was to "make regular."

The word trade can be substituted for commerce anywhere it is used in the Constitution, the Federalist Papers, the Constitutional Convention, and the State ratifying Conventions without changing the meaning. In an 1828 letter, James Madison made direct reference to the Commerce Clause and actually used the word trade in place of commerce.

As stated earlier, Congress may only exercise powers that provide for the defense or the welfare of the States. It has no power to provide for the welfare of the *citizens* directly. Under the category of "General Welfare," Congress is granted ten specific powers, each of which was designed to provide benefit to the States.

The context for delegating this specific power to Congress was the Confederation Period, when States were free to levy duties on products imported from other States. The purpose of granting the power to regulate trade that was conducted between the States was to ensure that trade flowed freely. In case the meaning was not clear enough, additional language was added in Article 1, Section 10, Clauses 2 and 3 **(C:1.10.2–3)**, where States are specifically prohibited from taxing imports or exports without permission from Congress.

For the first hundred years of our existence as a Union, that was exactly how the text was understood and applied. There was hardly ever a thought that regulate could mean "restrict." The first significant effort to limit interstate economic activity was not until 1887. The Interstate Commerce Act was an "Anti–Dog-Eat-Dog" law that was designed to stop railroads from what was perceived as price gouging and other practices that Congress deemed unfair.

The history of congressional action and High Court decisions since that time is voluminous. What becomes evident as one examines the time line is that Congress desired more power over trade (and later over manufacturing and farming), and that it was often limited or thwarted by Supreme Court decisions.

But over time, the Court began to yield, bringing us to the present day, when regulate commerce has come to mean "write any kind of law that requires anyone to do, or stop doing, anything, if the thing they are doing or not doing might affect themselves or anyone else." Interstate trade (or commerce) is the poster child for the Founders' fears that the

Government they called the "general government" would grow beyond its intended design.

> *Experience hath shewn, that even under the best forms*
> *[of government] those entrusted with power have, in time,*
> *and by slow operations, perverted it into tyranny. "*[28]
>
> —Thomas Jefferson, "Preamble to a Bill
> for the More General Diffusion
> of Knowledge," Fall 1778

The so-called "balance of powers" failed us for many reasons. One is that the balance was left between three branches of the same Government. All they had to do was agree on how to divide the spoils that were once State sovereignty and individual liberty.

Recently, however, Attorneys General, on behalf of at least twenty-six States, filed suit to hold the line against the new "Nationalized Medicine" program. If they succeed, or if the Supreme Court finds the law unconstitutional, the forces of tyranny will still be in our red zone; but kept, for now at least, from our end zone.

Necessary and Proper

> *A wise and frugal government, which shall . . . leave*
> *them otherwise free to regulate their own pursuits of*
> *industry and improvement, and shall not take from the*
> *mouth of labor the bread it has earned. This is*
> *the sum of good government.*[29]
>
> —Thomas Jefferson, First Inaugural Address,
> March 4, 1801

Of the three loopholes Congress has used over the years to expand its powers and strip us of the freedom to "regulate our own pursuits," perhaps the silliest and most transparent has been the use of the words "necessary and proper" from Article 1, Section 8, Clause 18 (**C:1.8.18**), to imply that Congress could enact any laws they felt were necessary or proper.

The first seventeen clauses of Section 8 grant Congress a clear list of powers under the categories of "Common Defense" and "General Welfare." The eighteenth clause does not grant *any* new power to Congress, let alone the "sweeping powers" they have often assumed under it. It is *not* an "elastic clause" as some are taught in law school, but merely an enablement, or implementation, clause:

> To make all Laws which shall be necessary and proper for carrying
> into Execution the foregoing Powers, and all other Powers vested by
> this Constitution in the Government of the United States, or in any
> Department or Officer thereof.

From the Constitutional Convention forward, these words meant exactly what any high school English teacher would construe them to mean. Congress was given the power to write laws that were necessary and proper in order to implement the powers just granted in Clauses 1 through 17. There was no new power being granted, except the power to write laws that turn the enumerated powers into action. If anything, the clause is restrictive. The words do not say that Congress may make any law it wishes as long as it references a foregoing power, but only if that law matches the additional description of being both necessary *and* proper.

As the original intent of the Founders to create a limited Federal Government fades into the past, and the intent of the current Government to replace it with an unlimited one looms in the present, it is worth noting the deliberateness and clarity with which the Founders spoke.

James Wilson from Pennsylvania is the man who proposed this clause at the Constitutional Convention. Even Madison and Hamilton may take a back seat for a moment, because no one would be more capable of interpreting James Wilson's own words than the man himself. At the Pennsylvania Ratifying Convention of December 1787, he explained that *the words he placed into the Constitution are*

> limited and defined by the following, "for carrying into execution the foregoing powers." It is saying no more than that the powers we have already particularly given, shall be effectually carried into execution.[30]

In "Federalist No. 33," Alexander Hamilton confirms this understanding. About these very words he stated that

> It may be affirmed with perfect confidence that the constitutional operation of the intended government would be precisely the same, if these clauses were entirely obliterated, as if they were repeated in every article. . . . The declaration itself, though it may be chargeable with tautology or redundancy, is at least perfectly harmless.[31]

Beginning with the 13th Amendment in 1865, Congress began to routinely do what Hamilton suggested might be done ("repeated [the clause] in every article"). They attached a lawmaking clause to nearly every Article of Amendment (except those that affected only Government operations, such as presidential terms and succession). These Amendments usually contain the following language:

> [The] Congress shall have power to enforce this article by appropriate legislation.

These implementation clauses did nothing to increase the power of Congress associated with each Amendment. Interestingly, no one ever has ever even tried to advance that argument. If these implementation clauses do not expand or enhance the powers with which they are associated in the case of Amendments, how would one reason that the "precedent" language in **C:1.8.18** does?

But it is not about reasoning, and certainly not about honoring the intent of the Founders. Our Founders knew that Governments tended to grow beyond any boundaries that liberty could abide. They wrote the Constitution to hinder that tendency. But for most of the history of our nation, most members of Congress, most Presidents, and most Supreme Court Justices have wanted to make "progress," as they defined it, and have actively exerted themselves against the boundaries they were sworn to honor, and therefore against their respective oaths.

A series of efforts by Congress to expand their powers on the basis of the words necessary and proper were at first rejected by the Supreme Court, then "progressively" permitted. Modern High Court decisions allow Congress to enact laws that are "plainly adapted" for carrying into execution their enumerated powers or are consistent with "the spirit of the Constitution." These vague boundaries are pretty far from original intent and getting farther every year.

> *How prone all human institutions have been to decay;*
> *how subject the best-formed and most wisely organized*
> *governments have been to lose their check and*
> *totally dissolve; how difficult it has been for mankind,*
> *in all ages and countries, to preserve their dearest rights*
> *and best privileges, impelled as it were*
> *by an irresistible fate of despotism.*[32]

—JAMES MONROE, VIRGINIA RATIFYING
CONVENTION, JUNE 10, 1788

Summary

The Declaration of Independence asserts that all humans are created equal, and that they are granted "rights" by their Creator as part of their humanness. Whenever Government, it says, becomes destructive of those rights, "it is the Right of the People to alter or to abolish it." Government should exist primarily to provide "Guards for their future security." Chief Justice Warren Burger called the Declaration of Independence "the promise," and the Constitution "its fulfillment."[33]

These five handwritten pages of parchment laid the framework for an experiment unique in all of history: the idea that humans should all live in liberty and that Government should be restrained, not (as in most countries for nearly all of history) the other way around. As our system was intended, individuals should be free to choose nearly every detail of their lives and accomplish as many of their goals and fulfill as many of their dreams as they can without help or interference from any Government. State capitals were designed to function as the seats of most administration, and the new "general Government" was to provide a common defense and certain other benefits to the member States.

The United States Constitution created a contract between sovereign States similar to the United Nations, the North Atlantic Treaty Organization, or the European Economic Community. It could also be properly called the original North American Free Trade Agreement (NAFTA). Each State had its own Constitution and its own Government, and had won its own independence from England; each of the thirteen States was named separately in the 1783 Treaty of Paris. In fact, the word State is deliberately capitalized in every instance in the Declaration of Independence—nine times referring to one or more of the United States, and once to the State of Great Britain. This was to signify that it was time for them to "assume among the powers of the earth, the separate and equal station to which the Laws of Nature and of Nature's God entitle them."

This capitalization is repeated 152 times in the Articles of Confederation (with only one unexplained exception), 210 times in the United States Constitution, including the Bill of Rights, and the other Amendments,[34] and over 1,500 times in the Federalist Papers, without exception. In fact, although the eighteenth century was a time of excessive capitalization of common nouns, the Federalist writers often used lowercase when referring to foreign states, but never to one or more of the United States.

The States were the building blocks of America. The States were once the Colonies that settled the New World. The States declared their Independence and fought the Revolution. The States formed the Confederation and wrote its Articles. The States were each granted independence from Britain. The States sent delegates to the Constitutional Convention. The States each separately ratified the Constitution and the Bill of Rights. Three-fourths of all States are still required in order to amend the Constitution. The States send delegates to both Houses of Congress,[35] and the States still elect the President.

Every State regarded itself as a nation and every other State as a separate nation until after the Civil War. Only then did Americans begin to use the singular verb to agree with the once-plural noun. Instead of saying, "The United States are . . ." it became accepted usage to say, "The United States is . . ." Until the Civil War, the question was not whether States had the authority to secede, but only whether such an extreme measure was necessary. The war answered that question by force, not by Constitutional argument. One result (often overlooked) was to degrade the sovereignty of the States and centralize power in Washington.

There were other major eras in the expansion of Federal power, such as the New Deal, the Great Society, the war on drugs, and the war on terror. Over time, small usurpations added up. George Washington had warned us about this effect in his Farewell Address:

If, in the opinion of the people, the distribution or modification of the constitutional powers be in any particular wrong, let it be corrected by an amendment in the way which the Constitution designates. But let there be no change by usurpation; for though this, in one instance, may be the instrument of good, it is the customary weapon by which free governments are destroyed. The precedent must always greatly overbalance in permanent evil any partial or transient benefit, which the use can at any time yield.[36]

Today, the States are hardly even states. They are no longer countries, but more aptly described as counties. Most schoolchildren do not know that the States formed the Federal Government instead of the other way around, and for all practical purposes it hardly matters. The Federal Government operates at this point as though the States were political subdivisions of its creation, little different from the counties and parishes within each State. The few powers granted to the three branches of the Federal Government by the Constitution have been replaced by a myriad of laws and regulations enforced by swarms of agencies that interfere with commerce and daily living, and are parasitic to the economy.

The nation, as we now refer to the fifty lowercase states, could fairly be renamed "The United State (singular) of America." At least the new subject-verb agreement would reflect good grammar and accurately reflect the current state of public affairs. This is truly a land far, far away from the Founders' intention, a literal reading of the Constitution, or a meaningful oath of office. In fact, as the author says publicly on frequent occasions, and without fear of serious contradiction, "The Government we have in Washington, D.C. today is the Government our founders feared, and wrote the Constitution to prevent."

We are very different today, but originalists do not believe that it is because the Constitution is living; on the contrary, because it is nearly dead. Over a hundred years of usurping powers not granted by the Constitution have resulted in a monstrous Government, with all three branches overgrowing their boundaries to the point where they are barely visible, and rarely referenced. Congress and the President seldom need to defend their actions. When asked about the constitutionality of the Patient Protection and Affordable Care Act, Nancy Pelosi replied, "Are you serious?" She repeated herself and then said, "That is not a serious question." Other Senators and Representatives simply say, "Of course it's constitutional!"—meaning that they have no idea.

Popular magazines treat the subject as if they know something about it, usually taking the Statist party line. In 2011, *Time* magazine (no less), on July 4 (no less), published a feature article by Richard Stengel in which he amazingly states:

> If the Constitution was intended to limit the federal government, it sure doesn't say so, Article 1, Section 8 . . . is a drumroll of congressional power. And it ends with the 'necessary and proper' clause."[37]

But even this does not match up to a *Washington Post* column, where supporters of the new health care reform characterize our great charter this way:

> The Constitution gives Congress the authority to "make all laws which shall be necessary and proper" to provide for the "general welfare."[38]

Wow! Combining these two misconstructions would certainly give Congress all the latitude they would need to write virtually any law whatsoever! This is not only the very definition of tyranny; it is sadly a sentiment many Americans would agree with (it is what they were taught), and with which very few would know how to intelligently disagree. We need to breathe new life back into our dying Constitution if we are to continue on the path of prosperity our Founders lighted for us. Every country in the world will always have problems. Jesus said we would always have some poor people with us, and that has never been otherwise in a single city in any country ever in the history of the world. There will always be illness and aging. Most families will have at least some turmoil. But the kinds of problems that Government can affect have either been caused by or exacerbated when America has neglected her Constitution. And every one of these same ills can be cured or dramatically improved by returning to it.

It may be fair to say that freedom in the world for the future as far as we can fathom may be determined by the answer to a single question: Will Government, any Government, ever have limits—any limits—on its power, or will every Government eventually exercise unlimited control over the people within its borders? Our Founders understood history, and addressed this question as they crafted a new framework for freedom. But the direction in which America has moved steadily, and sometimes rapidly, for decades, is toward the same sort of tyranny that most countries have endured for thousands of years. The powers that Congress has usurped have been "ratcheting" steadily forward. Thousands of laws are written, a few are challenged, but very few are ever struck down. There are multitudes of new regulations added every year.[39]

Woodrow Wilson commented on this phenomenon in *Congressional Government*:

CONGRESS always makes what haste it can to legislate. It is the prime object of its rules to expedite law-making. . . . Be the matters small or great, frivolous or grave, which busy it, its aim is to have laws always a-making.[40]

Does anything, or anyone stand in the way? Yes, *you* do! That is why you must understand the United States Constitution. In your hands it may be a tool, or even a weapon, to defend the freedoms our Founders wrote the Constitution to protect. Our elected and appointed officials in every State, and in the United States, still take an oath to "support and defend the Constitution of the United States" and to "bear true faith and allegiance" to it. It is up to you to hold their feet to that fire! We can, in the immortal words of William F. Buckley, "Stand athwart history, yelling Stop!"[41]

Politicians often patronize us and tell us not to worry our pretty little heads about such things, that we can trust them to look after our freedoms. *But it was to prevent them from deciding the limits on their own power that the Constitution was created!* "We, the people" are the ones who must defend *our* liberties from *their* encroachment. They often claim to have good intentions, and sometimes they may. But Daniel Webster put the nail in that coffin when he said,

> Good intentions will always be pleaded for any assumption of power. . . .
> The Constitution was made to guard the people against the dangers of
> good intention, real or pretended. . . . There are men in all ages who . . .
> mean to govern well, but they mean to govern. They promise to be kind
> masters, but they mean to be masters.[42]

Free men and women do not have masters. You, Dear Reader, are charged by virtue of your citizenship to defend the unalienable rights granted to you and your children by your Creator. Push back, and **demand** that your public servants honor their oath.

Accept responsibility for your own life, and teach that central precept as the very moral code of liberty. Take care of others who are in need as you are able, and join together with religious organizations and charities that do the same. Do not let any Government do for you and those around you what you know in your heart you ought to do for yourself, and for them. If you must accept charity, look first to family, friends, and religious and charitable organizations. They will not take your freedom in trade.

Find free-market solutions to the problems society faces. Leave some problems unsolved, rather than letting Government make them worse at your expense.

Vote for candidates at every level who understand what you are reading now and make them prove their faithfulness to it. Support your State in every effort it exerts against Federal encroachment. The liberties of American citizens, and the sovereignty of the member States, will never be jeopardized by a much smaller Federal budget, fewer Federal laws, or too high a regard for direct constitutional authority.

John Jay, our first Chief Justice, said that every citizen ought to study the Constitution so that he would know when his rights were being violated and be better prepared to defend them. If the boundaries on Government are not found here, then where are they? How can we be sure that a Government without these boundaries will ever respect any limitations at all? How can we be assured that the rights of all minorities will be protected? If there are no boundaries on Government, there are no sureties for liberty. How can we be certain that even the freedoms of speech and the press will not be trampled? Officials who will not honor the boundaries that they swore to support and defend can certainly not be trusted to set their own limits.

The price of freedom is eternal vigilance—not just against invasion from without, but more especially from usurpers and power freaks from within. Since the freedom of the next generation of Americans (and more) is in the balance, why not begin today to understand the contract that enabled this great country of ours to get into motion? Once you understand it, you will be better prepared to defend it. The best place your humble author can think of to start is by reading and turning the few pages that follow.

The preservation of the sacred fire of liberty, and the destiny of the Republican model of Government, are justly considered as deeply, perhaps as finally staked, on the experiment entrusted to the hands of the American people.

—George Washington, First Inaugural Address, April 30, 1789[43]

UNITED STATES
CONSTITUTION

Side-by-Side—

THE CONSTITUTION
MADE EASY

Constitution of the United States

We the People of the United States, in Order to form a more perfect Union, establish Justice, insure domestic Tranquility, provide for the common defence, promote the general Welfare, and secure the Blessings of Liberty to ourselves and our Posterity, do ordain and establish this Constitution for the United States of America.

Article. I.

Section. 1.

All legislative Powers herein granted shall be vested in a Congress of the United States, which shall consist of a Senate and House of Representatives.

Section. 2.

The House of Representatives shall be composed of Members chosen every second Year by the People of the several States, and the Electors in each State shall have the Qualifications requisite for Electors of the most numerous Branch of the State Legislature.

No Person shall be a Representative who shall not have attained to the Age of twenty five Years, and been seven Years a Citizen of the United States, and who shall not, when elected, be an Inhabitant of that State in which he shall be chosen.

<u>Representatives and direct Taxes shall be apportioned among the several States which may be included within this Union, according to their respective Numbers, which shall be determined by adding to the whole Number of free Persons, including those bound to Service for a Term of Years, and excluding Indians not taxed, three fifths of all other Persons.</u> [Changed by Section 2 of the 14th Amendment, and the 16th Amendment]

THE CONSTITUTION OF THE UNITED STATES

We the people of the United States, have created and agreed to this Constitution for the United States of America. We have done this in order to make our Union stronger, set standards for justice, keep the peace at home, provide for our common defense, promote our general well-being, and make sure that the blessings of liberty continue for ourselves and our descendents.

Article 1

SECTION 1

1.1.1 All of the lawmaking Powers granted by this agreement will be entrusted to a Congress of the United States. Congress will consist of a Senate and a House of Representatives.

SECTION 2

1.2.1 The members of the House of Representatives will be elected every two years by the people in each of the States. Each State has a standard it uses to decide who is allowed to vote[1] for its own State legislature.[2] This same standard must be used to determine who is allowed to vote for members of the House of Representatives.

1.2.2 A Representative must be at least twenty-five years old, and a citizen of the United States for seven years. At the time he or she[3] is elected, the Representative must be a resident of the State that elected him or her.

1.2.3a[4] The number of Representatives that each State has will be based upon the population of that State. So will direct taxes (except for income tax.)[5] For these purposes the population will count everybody except tax-exempt American Indians [who live and work on reservations]. The right to vote may not be denied to any citizen in any State who is at least eighteen years old.[6] This includes the right to vote for President and Vice President[7] of the United States, Representatives in Congress, as well as the Governor, judges and legislators of that State. If any State prevents or hinders any eligible person from voting, unless that person participated in rebellion or other crime, the number of Representatives that State is entitled to will be reduced in proportion. [From **A:14.2** and **A:16**]

ARTICLE. I.

The actual Enumeration shall be made within three Years after the first Meeting of the Congress of the United States, and within every subsequent Term of ten Years, in such Manner as they shall by Law direct. The Number of Representatives shall not exceed one for every thirty Thousand, but each State shall have at Least one Representative; and until such enumeration shall be made, the State of New Hampshire shall be entitled to chuse three, Massachusetts eight, Rhode-Island and Providence Plantations one, Connecticut five, New-York six, New Jersey four, Pennsylvania eight, Delaware one, Maryland six, Virginia ten, North Carolina five, South Carolina five, and Georgia three.

When vacancies happen in the Representation from any State, the Executive Authority thereof shall issue Writs of Election to fill such Vacancies.

The House of Representatives shall chuse their Speaker and other Officers; and shall have the sole Power of Impeachment.

SECTION. 3.

The Senate of the United States shall be composed of two Senators from each State, chosen by the Legislature thereof for six Years; and each Senator shall have one Vote. [Changed by the 17th Amendment]

Immediately after they shall be assembled in Consequence of the first Election, they shall be divided as equally as may be into three Classes. The Seats of the Senators of the first Class shall be vacated at the Expiration of the second Year, of the second Class at the Expiration of the fourth Year, and of the third Class at the Expiration of the sixth Year, so that one third may be chosen every second Year;

and if Vacancies happen by Resignation, or otherwise, during the Recess of the Legislature of any State, the Executive thereof may make temporary Appointments until the next Meeting of the Legislature, which shall then fill such Vacancies. [Changed by the 17th Amendment]

1.2.3b The actual census must be taken within three years after the first meeting of the Congress of the United States, and every ten years after that. Congress will determine by Law how the census will be taken. Each State will have at least one Representative, but otherwise not more than one for each thirty-thousand people.[8] Until the first census is taken, the number of Representatives from each State will be New Hampshire three, Massachusetts eight, Rhode Island one, Connecticut five, New York six, New Jersey four, Pennsylvania eight, Delaware one, Maryland six, Virginia ten, North Carolina five, South Carolina five, and Georgia three.

1.2.4 When any Representative does not finish his or her term, the Governor from his or her State must appoint someone for the remainder of that term.

1.2.5 The House of Representatives will choose their Speaker and other officers, and will have the exclusive Power to bring a charge of impeachment.[9]

SECTION 3

1.3.1[10] The Senate of the United States will consist of two Senators from each State, elected by the people of that State for six years; and each Senator will have one vote. Each State has a standard it uses to decide who is allowed to vote[11] for its own State legislature. This same standard must be used to determine who is allowed to vote for members of the Senate. [From **A:17.a**]

1.3.2a After the first election of Senators, and as soon they meet for the first time, they will be divided into three groups. The first term of the first group will end in two years; the first term of the second group will end in four years; and the first term of the third group will end in six years. In this way, one third of the Senate will be elected every two years.

1.3.2b[12] When any Senator does not finish his or her term, the Governor from his or her State must set a Special Election to fill the remainder of that term. However, the legislature of that State may give the Governor Power to make a temporary appointment that will only last until the position is filled by the Special Election. [From **A:17.b**]

SECTION. 3. (CONTINUED)

No Person shall be a Senator who shall not have attained to the Age of thirty Years, and been nine Years a Citizen of the United States, and who shall not, when elected, be an Inhabitant of that State for which he shall be chosen.

The Vice President of the United States shall be President of the Senate, but shall have no Vote, unless they be equally divided.

The Senate shall chuse their other Officers, and also a President pro tempore, in the Absence of the Vice President, or when he shall exercise the Office of President of the United States.

The Senate shall have the sole Power to try all Impeachments. When sitting for that Purpose, they shall be on Oath or Affirmation. When the President of the United States is tried, the Chief Justice shall preside: And no Person shall be convicted without the Concurrence of two thirds of the Members present.

Judgment in Cases of Impeachment shall not extend further than to removal from Office, and disqualification to hold and enjoy any Office of honor, Trust or Profit under the United States: but the Party convicted shall nevertheless be liable and subject to Indictment, Trial, Judgment and Punishment, according to Law.

SECTION. 4.

The Times, Places and Manner of holding Elections for Senators and Representatives, shall be prescribed in each State by the Legislature thereof; but the Congress may at any time by Law make or alter such Regulations, except as to the Places of chusing Senators.

The Congress shall assemble at least once in every Year, and such Meeting shall be on the first Monday in December, unless they shall by Law appoint a different Day. [Changed by the 20th Amendment]

SECTION. 5.

Each House shall be the Judge of the Elections, Returns and Qualifications of its own Members, and a Majority of each shall constitute a Quorum to

1.3.3 A Senator must be at least thirty years old, and a citizen of the United States for nine years. At the time he or she is elected, the Senator must be a resident of the State that elected him or her.

1.3.4 The Vice President of the United States will be President[13] of the Senate, but may not vote except to break a tie.

1.3.5 The Senate will choose their other officers, and also a temporary[14] President. He or she will preside[15] only if the Vice President is absent, or when the Vice President is the Acting President of the United States.

1.3.6 The Senate will have the exclusive Power to try all impeachments.[16] When Senators are conducting an impeachment trial, they must first swear that they will act impartially.[17] When the President of the United States is tried, the Chief Justice will preside. There will be no conviction unless two-thirds of the members present vote for it.

1.3.7 The most serious consequences of impeachment will be to remove the person from office, and disqualify him or her from holding any official position under the United States. However, a convicted person may still have other liability, and could be charged, tried, judged, and punished according to Law.[18]

SECTION 4

1.4.1 The times, places, and methods of holding elections for Senators and Representatives will be decided by each State legislature. Congress may override these regulations at any time by Law.[19]

1.4.2 The terms of Congress will end at noon on January 3, and the terms of their successors will then begin. Congress must meet at least once in every year, and that meeting will also begin at noon on January 3, unless that date is changed by Law.[20] [From **A:20.2**]

SECTION 5

1.5.1 Each House will decide its own elections, returns (ballot result reports), and qualifications of its own members. Each House must have a majority present for there to be a quorum[21] that can do business. But a smaller do Business; but a smaller Number may adjourn from day to day, and may be authorized to compel the Attendance of absent Members, in such Manner, and under such Penalties as each House may provide.

Each House may determine the Rules of its Proceedings, punish its Members for disorderly Behaviour, and, with the Concurrence of two thirds, expel a Member.

Each House shall keep a Journal of its Proceedings, and from time to time publish the same, excepting such Parts as may in their Judgment require Secrecy; and the Yeas and Nays of the Members of either House on any question shall, at the Desire of one fifth of those Present, be entered on the Journal.

Neither House, during the Session of Congress, shall, without the Consent of the other, adjourn for more than three days, nor to any other Place than that in which the two Houses shall be sitting.

Section. 6.

The Senators and Representatives shall receive a Compensation for their Services, to be ascertained by Law, and paid out of the Treasury of the United States.

They shall in all Cases, except Treason, Felony and Breach of the Peace, be privileged from Arrest during their Attendance at the Session of their respective Houses, and in going to and returning from the same; and for any Speech or Debate in either House, they shall not be questioned in any other Place.

No Senator or Representative shall, during the Time for which he was elected, be appointed to any civil Office under the Authority of the United States, which shall have been created, or the Emoluments whereof shall have been encreased during such time; and no Person holding any Office under the United States, shall be a Member of either House during his Continuance in Office.

Section. 7.

All Bills for raising Revenue shall originate in the House of Representatives; but the Senate may propose or concur with Amendments as on other Bills.

number may meet and then adjourn[22] each day, and may be authorized to make the absent members attend. Each House may decide how members can be made to attend, or penalized for not attending.

1.5.2 Each House may decide the rules of its proceedings, punish its members for disorderly conduct, and expel a member by a two-thirds vote.

1.5.3 Each House must keep a journal (records) of its proceedings and periodically publish it, but may omit certain parts that are deemed to require secrecy. One-fifth of those present in either House may require that the "Yes" and "No" votes of the members on any question be recorded in the journal.

1.5.4 When Congress is in session, neither House may adjourn for more than three days without the consent of the other House. The same consent will be required for either House to adjourn to any other location.

SECTION 6

1.6.1a Senators and Representatives must be paid for their services in an amount set by Law, and paid out of the Treasury of the United States. Any change in their pay will not take effect until after the next election of Representatives.[23]

1.6.1b No Senator or Representative may be arrested while they are attending a session of their respective Houses, or while they are going to or returning from a session, except for treason, felony or disturbing the peace.[24] Further, they may not be arrested because of any speech or debate in either House, and they may not be questioned in any other place.

1.6.2 No Senator or Representative may be appointed to any official position under the authority of the United States during their term in office if that position was created during their term or if the pay plan for that position was increased during their term. No person holding any official position in the U.S. Government may be a member of either House at the same time that he or she holds this other office.

SECTION 7

1.7.1 All bills for raising money must originate in the House of Representatives. But the Senate may propose or agree with amendments to these bills, just as it can with other bills.

Every Bill which shall have passed the House of Representatives and the Senate, shall, before it become a Law, be presented to the President of the United States: If he approve he shall sign it, but if not he shall return it, with his Objections to that House in which it shall have originated, who shall enter the Objections at large on their Journal, and proceed to reconsider it.

If after such Reconsideration two thirds of that House shall agree to pass the Bill, it shall be sent, together with the Objections, to the other House, by which it shall likewise be reconsidered, and if approved by two thirds of that House, it shall become a Law.

But in all such Cases the Votes of both Houses shall be determined by yeas and Nays, and the Names of the Persons voting for and against the Bill shall be entered on the Journal of each House respectively. If any Bill shall not be returned by the President within ten Days (Sundays excepted) after it shall have been presented to him, the Same shall be a Law, in like Manner as if he had signed it, unless the Congress by their Adjournment prevent its Return, in which Case it shall not be a Law.

Every Order, Resolution, or Vote to which the Concurrence of the Senate and House of Representatives may be necessary (except on a question of Adjournment) shall be presented to the President of the United States; and before the Same shall take Effect, shall be approved by him, or being disapproved by him, shall be repassed by two thirds of the Senate and House of Representatives, according to the Rules and Limitations prescribed in the Case of a Bill.

SECTION. 8.

The Congress shall have Power

To lay and collect Taxes, Duties, Imposts and Excises, to pay the Debts and provide for the common Defence and general Welfare of the United States; but all Duties, Imposts and Excises shall be uniform throughout the United States;

To borrow Money on the credit of the United States;

1.7.2a Every bill that passes the House and Senate must be presented to the President of the United States before it becomes a Law. If the President approves of it, he or she must sign it. If not, the President must return it, along with his or her objections, to the House in which it originated. That House must enter the President's objections in its records, and proceed to reconsider it.

1.7.2b After they reconsider, if two-thirds of that House agrees to pass the bill, it must be sent, together with the objections, to the other House. That House must also reconsider it, and if they approve it by a two-thirds vote, it will become a Law.

1.7.2c In all such cases, the votes of both Houses must be determined by saying "Yes" or "No," and the names of the people voting for and against the bill must be entered in the records of each House respectively. If any bill is not returned by the President within ten days after it has been presented to him or her (not counting Sundays), it will become a Law, just as if he or she had signed it. There is an exception if Congress adjourns in less than ten days, which prevents its return, in which case it will not become Law.

1.7.3 Every other kind of order, resolution, or vote which the Senate and the House of Representatives have to both agree on, must be presented to the President of the United States. Before it can take effect, it must be approved by him or her. If the President does not approve it, it must be re-passed by two-thirds of the Senate and House of Representatives in order for it to go into effect. The same rules and limitations apply as in the case of a bill (see above), but do not apply to a vote to adjourn.

SECTION 8
Congress will have Power:

1.8.1 To assess and collect taxes on imports, exports, and purchases to pay the debts and provide for the common defense and general well-being[25] of the United States. All such taxes must be uniform[26] throughout the United States;

1.8.2 To borrow money on the credit of the United States;

ARTICLE. I.

To regulate Commerce with foreign Nations, and among the several States, and with the Indian Tribes;

To establish an uniform Rule of Naturalization, and uniform Laws on the subject of Bankruptcies throughout the United States;

To coin Money, regulate the Value thereof, and of foreign Coin, and fix the Standard of Weights and Measures;

To provide for the Punishment of counterfeiting the Securities and current Coin of the United States;

To establish Post Offices and post Roads;

To promote the Progress of Science and useful Arts, by securing for limited Times to Authors and Inventors the exclusive Right to their respective Writings and Discoveries;

To constitute Tribunals inferior to the supreme Court;

To define and punish Piracies and Felonies committed on the high Seas, and Offences against the Law of Nations;

To declare War, grant Letters of Marque and Reprisal, and make Rules concerning Captures on Land and Water;

To raise and support Armies, but no Appropriation of Money to that Use shall be for a longer Term than two Years;

To provide and maintain a Navy;

To make Rules for the Government and Regulation of the land and naval Forces;

To provide for calling forth the Militia to execute the Laws of the Union, suppress Insurrections and repel Invasions;

1.8.3 To regulate trade with foreign nations, and among the separate States, and with the Indian tribes;

1.8.4 To establish standard rules for becoming a naturalized citizen,[27] and establish standard Laws about bankruptcy throughout the United States;

1.8.5 To coin money, decide the value of it, decide the value of foreign currency, and set the standard of weights and measures;

1.8.6 To decide the punishment for counterfeiting the money and other valuables of the United States;

1.8.7 To establish post offices and post roads;

1.8.8 To promote the progress of science and useful arts by making sure that authors and inventors have ownership of their writings and discoveries for a certain period of time;

1.8.9 To create lower courts under the Supreme Court;

1.8.10 To define and punish piracy, felonies committed on the high seas, and international crimes;

1.8.11 To declare war, grant letters of retaliation,[28] and make rules concerning captures[29] on land and water;

1.8.12 To raise and support Armies—however, Congress may not allocate money for this purpose for more than two years at a time;

1.8.13 To provide and maintain a Navy;

1.8.14 To make rules that govern and regulate the land and naval forces;

1.8.15 To provide for calling upon the Militia[30] to enforce the Laws of the Union, put down rebellions, and repel invasions;

SECTION. 8. (CONTINUED)

To provide for organizing, arming, and disciplining, the Militia, and for governing such Part of them as may be employed in the Service of the United States, reserving to the States respectively, the Appointment of the Officers, and the Authority of training the Militia according to the discipline prescribed by Congress;

To exercise exclusive Legislation in all Cases whatsoever, over such District (not exceeding ten Miles square) as may, by Cession of particular States, and the Acceptance of Congress, become the Seat of the Government of the United States, and to exercise like Authority over all Places purchased by the Consent of the Legislature of the State in which the Same shall be, for the Erection of Forts, Magazines, Arsenals, dock-Yards, and other needful Buildings;—And

To make all Laws which shall be necessary and proper for carrying into Execution the foregoing Powers, and all other Powers vested by this Constitution in the Government of the United States, or in any Department or Officer thereof.

SECTION. 9.

The Migration or Importation of such Persons as any of the States now existing shall think proper to admit, shall not be prohibited by the Congress prior to the Year one thousand eight hundred and eight, but a Tax or duty may be imposed on such Importation, not exceeding ten dollars for each Person.

The Privilege of the Writ of Habeas Corpus shall not be suspended, unless when in Cases of Rebellion or Invasion the public Safety may require it.

No Bill of Attainder or ex post facto Law shall be passed.

No Capitation, or other direct, Tax shall be laid, unless in Proportion to the Census or enumeration herein before directed to be taken. [Changed by the 16th Amendment]

No Tax or Duty shall be laid on Articles exported from any State.

No Preference shall be given by any Regulation of Commerce or Revenue to the Ports of one State over those of another; nor shall Vessels bound to, or from, one State, be obliged to enter, clear, or pay Duties in another.

1.8.16 To provide for organizing, arming, and disciplining the Militia, and for governing any Militia members who are serving the United States at the time. The States will still appoint the officers, and have the authority to train the Militia according to the standards prescribed by Congress;

1.8.17 To make all Laws whatsoever for the District that will be the headquarters of the Government of the United States (Washington, D.C.).[31] This District will not be more than ten miles square, and will consist of land granted by one or more States and accepted by Congress. Congress will have the same authority over forts, storage places for weapons and ammunition, dockyards,[32] and other necessary buildings. These places must first be purchased with the consent of the legislature of the State where they are located; and

1.8.18 To make all Laws which are necessary and proper for executing the Powers listed above, and all other Powers granted by this Constitution to the Government of the United States, or to any department or officer of it.

SECTION 9[33]

1.9.1 The existing States may allow any people they wish to be admitted or imported. Congress may not prohibit this before the year 1808, but may impose a tax of up to ten dollars per person. [This clause was changed by Law on January 1, 1808.][34]

1.9.2 The right of any arrested person to be seen by an impartial judge[35] may not be suspended. There may be exceptions only during a rebellion or invasion if public safety requires it.

1.9.3 No Law may be passed that pronounces a person guilty of a crime,[36] or that is retroactive.[37]

1.9.4 No direct taxes may be assessed unless they are in proportion to the census. There is an exception for income tax.[38] [From **A:16**]

1.9.5 No tax may be assessed on goods exported from any State.

1.9.6 No preference may be given to the ports of one State over those of another by regulating the trade or taxes. Ships bound to or from one State, may not be required to enter, stop at, or pay taxes in another.

ARTICLE 1

SECTION. 9. (CONTINUED)

No Money shall be drawn from the Treasury, but in Consequence of Appropriations made by Law; and a regular Statement and Account of the Receipts and Expenditures of all public Money shall be published from time to time.

No Title of Nobility shall be granted by the United States: And no Person holding any Office of Profit or Trust under them, shall, without the Consent of the Congress, accept of any present, Emolument, Office, or Title, of any kind whatever, from any King, Prince, or foreign State.

SECTION. 10.

No State shall enter into any Treaty, Alliance, or Confederation; grant Letters of Marque and Reprisal;

coin Money; emit Bills of Credit; make any Thing but gold and silver Coin a Tender in Payment of Debts;

pass any Bill of Attainder, ex post facto Law,

or Law impairing the Obligation of Contracts, or grant any Title of Nobility.

No State shall, without the Consent of the Congress, lay any Imposts or Duties on Imports or Exports, except what may be absolutely necessary for executing it's inspection Laws: and the net Produce of all Duties and Imposts, laid by any State on Imports or Exports, shall be for the Use of the Treasury of the United States; and all such Laws shall be subject to the Revision and Controul of the Congress.

No State shall, without the Consent of Congress, lay any Duty of Tonnage, keep Troops, or Ships of War in time of Peace, enter into any Agreement or Compact with another State, or with a foreign Power, or engage in War, unless actually invaded, or in such imminent Danger as will not admit of delay.

1.9.7 No money may be taken out of the Treasury, except the amounts that have been allocated by Law. Financial statements that show all income and expenses must be made available to the public on a regular basis.

1.9.8 No title of nobility may be granted by the United States.[39] No person who holds any official position under them may accept any gift, money, office, or title of any kind from any king, prince, or foreign State without the consent of Congress.

SECTION 10[40]

1.10.1a No State may enter into any treaty, alliance, or confederation; neither may it grant letters of retaliation.[41]

1.10.1b (No State may) coin money, print paper money, or make anything except gold and silver coin a method of paying debts.

1.10.1c (No State may) pass any Law that pronounces a person guilty of a crime,[42] or that is retroactive.[43]

1.10.1d (No State may) pass any Law that interferes with private contracts, or grant any title of nobility.

1.10.2 The consent of Congress is required before any State may assess any tax on imports or exports, except what is absolutely necessary for executing its inspection Laws. The net proceeds of all these taxes will be for the use of the Treasury of the United States, and all such Laws will be subject to the revision and control of Congress.

1.10.3 The consent of Congress is required before any State may assess any tax based on the weight of shipments, or keep troops or warships in time of peace, or enter into any agreement or compact with another State or foreign Power, or engage in war. There is an exception for engaging in war if a State is actually invaded, or is in such immediate danger that it does not dare to wait.

Article. II.

SECTION. 1.

The executive Power shall be vested in a President of the United States of America. He shall hold his Office during the term of four Years, and, together with the Vice President, chosen for the same term, be elected, as follows:

Each State shall appoint, in such Manner as the Legislature thereof may direct, a Number of Electors, equal to the whole Number of Senators and Representatives to which the State may be entitled in the Congress: but no Senator or Representative, or Person holding an Office of Trust or Profit under the United States, shall be appointed an Elector.

The Electors shall meet in their respective States, and vote by Ballot for two Persons, of whom one at least shall not be an Inhabitant of the same State with themselves. [Changed by the 12th Amendment]

And they shall make a List of all the Persons voted for, and of the Number of Votes for each; which List they shall sign and certify, and transmit sealed to the Seat of the Government of the United States, directed to the President of the Senate. [Changed by the 12th Amendment]

The President of the Senate shall, in the Presence of the Senate and House of Representatives, open all the Certificates, and the Votes shall then be counted. The Person having the greatest Number of Votes shall be the President, if such Number be a Majority of the whole Number of Electors appointed; [Changed by the 12th Amendment]

and if there be more than one who have such Majority, and have an equal Number of Votes, then the House of Representatives shall immediately chuse by Ballot one of them for President; and if no Person have a Majority, then from the five highest on the List the said House shall in like Manner chuse the President. But in chusing the President, the Votes shall be taken by States, the Representation from each State having one Vote; A quorum for this purpose shall consist of a Member or Members from two thirds of the States, and a Majority of all the States shall be necessary to a Choice. [Changed by the 12th Amendment]

Article 2

SECTION 1

2.1.1 The executive Power will be entrusted to a President of the United States of America. He or she will hold his or her office for a term of four years, not to exceed two terms.[44] Each term will begin and end at noon on January 20.[45] The President and Vice President will be elected to the same term as follows:

2.1.2 Each State (and Washington, D.C.)[46] must appoint a number of electors equal to the total number of Senators and Representatives which that State (or District) is entitled to in Congress. The legislature of each State may determine the manner in which the electors are chosen. No Senator or Representative, or person holding an official position under the United States, may be appointed as an elector.

2.1.3a[47] The electors must meet in their respective States, and vote by ballot for President and Vice President. They may not vote for a President and a Vice President who are both residents of the same State as the electors. [From **A:12a**]

2.1.3b They must name in one set of ballots the person they voted for as President, and in a different set of ballots the person they voted for as Vice President. They must make separate lists of all the persons they voted for as President, and of all persons they voted for as Vice President, and the number of votes for each. They must sign these lists, and certify that they are correct, and send them sealed to the President of the Senate. [From **A:12b**]

2.1.3c. The President of the Senate must open all the certificates in the presence of the Senate and House of Representatives, and the votes must then be counted. The person receiving the greatest number of votes for President will become the President, as long as he or she receives a majority of the total number of electors. [From **A:12c**]

2.1.3d If no person receives a majority, then the House of Representatives must immediately elect the President by ballot. They must choose him or her from the three persons with the highest numbers of votes. In choosing the President, the votes must be taken by States, and each State will have one vote. A quorum for this purpose will consist of at least one member from two-thirds of the States, and a majority of all the States will be necessary for the election to be final. [From **A:12d**]

[See Section 3 of Amendment 20]

Article. II.

[See Section 3 of Amendment 20]

In every Case, after the Choice of the President, the Person having the greatest Number of Votes of the Electors shall be the Vice President. But if there should remain two or more who have equal Votes, the Senate shall chuse from them by Ballot the Vice President. [Changed by the 12th Amendment]

The Congress may determine the Time of chusing the Electors, and the Day on which they shall give their Votes; which Day shall be the same throughout the United States.

No Person except a natural born Citizen, or a Citizen of the United States, at the time of the Adoption of this Constitution, shall be eligible to the Office of President; neither shall any Person be eligible to that Office who shall not have attained to the Age of thirty five Years, and been fourteen Years a Resident within the United States.

In Case of the Removal of the President from Office, or of his Death, Resignation, or Inability to discharge the Powers and Duties of the said Office, the Same shall devolve on the Vice President, [Changed by the 25th Amendment]

[See Amendment 25]

and the Congress may by Law provide for the Case of Removal, Death, Resignation or Inability, both of the President and Vice President, declaring

2.1.3e If the President-elect dies before the beginning of his or her term (noon, January 20), then the Vice President–elect will become President. If a President has not been chosen before the beginning of his or her term, or if the President-elect does not qualify, then the Vice President–elect will act as President until a qualified President is chosen. [From **A:12e** and **A:20.3a**]

2.1.3f In case neither a President-elect nor a Vice President–elect qualifies, Congress may provide for this by Law. This Law will determine who will act as President, or the way in which the Acting President will be selected. This person will act as President until a qualified President or Vice President is chosen. [From **A:12f** and **A:20.3b**]

2.1.3g The person receiving the greatest number of votes for Vice President will become the Vice President, as long as he or she receives a majority of the total number of electors. If no person receives a majority, then the Senate must choose the Vice President between the two persons with the highest numbers of votes. A quorum for this purpose will consist of two-thirds of the total number of Senators, and a majority of the total number will be necessary for the election to be final. If a person is not eligible under the Constitution to be President of the United States, that person will not be eligible to be Vice President either. [From **A:12g**]

2.1.4 Congress may determine the time of choosing the electors, and the day on which they must cast their votes. This day must be the same throughout the United States.

2.1.5 To be eligible for the office of President, a person must be a natural-born citizen, or else a citizen at the time this Constitution was adopted. He or she must also be at least thirty-five years old and a resident within the United States for at least fourteen years.

2.1.6a[48] In case of the removal of the President from office, or of his or her death or resignation, the Vice President will become President. [From **A:25.1**]

2.1.6b Whenever there is a vacancy in the office of the Vice President, the President must nominate a new Vice President. This person will take office upon confirmation by a majority vote of both Houses of Congress. [From **A:25.2**]

2.1.6c In case the President and Vice President are both removed from office, or have died, or have resigned, or have become unable to discharge

ARTICLE 2

ARTICLE. II.

what Officer shall then act as President, and such Officer shall act
accordingly, until the Disability be removed, or a President shall be elected.
*[Note: The whole paragraph above was underlined in the original; but a portion
has been retained in this version as there is no replacement language in the 25th
Amendment or any other Amendment. See 2.1.6c and endnote.]*

[See Amendment 25]

[See Amendment 25]

[See Amendment 25]

[See Amendment 25]

The President shall, at stated Times, receive for his Services, a
Compensation, which shall neither be increased nor diminished during the
Period for which he shall have been elected, and he shall not receive within
that Period any other Emolument from the United States, or any of them.

the powers and duties of office, Congress may provide for this by Law. This Law will determine who will act as President until the existing President or Vice President is able to resume office, or until a new President is elected.[49]

2.1.6d Whenever the President believes that he or she is unable to discharge the powers and duties of office, he or she may send written declaration to the temporary President of the Senate and to the Speaker of the House of Representatives. Until the President sends them a written declaration that he or she has become able again, these powers and duties must be discharged by the Vice President as Acting President. [From **A:25.3**]

2.1.6e Whenever the Vice President and a majority of the Cabinet, or some other group Congress designates by Law,[50] agree that the President is unable to discharge the powers and duties of office, they may send their written declaration to the temporary President of the Senate and the Speaker of the House of Representatives. Then the Vice President must immediately assume the powers and duties as Acting President. [From **A:25.4**]

2.1.6f If, in response, the President believes that no inability exists, he or she must send written declaration to the temporary President of the Senate and to the Speaker of the House of Representatives. The President will then resume the powers and duties of office unless the Vice President and a majority of the Cabinet officers oppose him or her. If they do, they must send their written declaration within four days to the temporary President of the Senate and to the Speaker of the House of Representatives, reasserting that the President is unable to discharge the powers and duties of office. [From **A:25.4.2a**]

2.1.6g At this point Congress must decide the issue. They must meet within forty-eight hours for this purpose if they are not already in session. Congress must make a determination within twenty-one days of receiving the most recent declaration (or twenty-three days if they were not in session). If Congress determines that the President is unable to discharge the powers and duties of office, then the Vice President will continue as Acting President. This must be done by two-thirds vote of both Houses. Otherwise, the President will resume the powers and duties of his or her office. [From **A:25.4.2b**]

2.1.7 The President must be paid on a regular basis. This pay may not be increased nor decreased during his or her term in office. During this term, the President may not receive any other payment from the United States, or any of them (either the Federal Government or any State Government).

Before he enter on the Execution of his Office, he shall take the following Oath or Affirmation:--"I do solemnly swear (or affirm) that I will faithfully execute the Office of President of the United States, and will to the best of my Ability, preserve, protect and defend the Constitution of the United States."

ARTICLE. II.

SECTION. 2.

The President shall be Commander in Chief of the Army and Navy of the United States, and of the Militia of the several States, when called into the actual Service of the United States; he may require the Opinion, in writing, of the principal Officer in each of the executive Departments, upon any Subject relating to the Duties of their respective Offices, and he shall have Power to grant Reprieves and Pardons for Offences against the United States, except in Cases of Impeachment.

He shall have Power, by and with the Advice and Consent of the Senate, to make Treaties, provided two thirds of the Senators present concur; and he shall nominate, and by and with the Advice and Consent of the Senate, shall appoint Ambassadors, other public Ministers and Consuls, Judges of the supreme Court, and all other Officers of the United States, whose Appointments are not herein otherwise provided for, and which shall be established by Law:

but the Congress may by Law vest the Appointment of such inferior Officers, as they think proper, in the President alone, in the Courts of Law, or in the Heads of Departments.

The President shall have Power to fill up all Vacancies that may happen during the Recess of the Senate, by granting Commissions which shall expire at the End of their next Session.

SECTION. 3.

He shall from time to time give to the Congress Information of the State of the Union, and recommend to their Consideration such Measures as he shall judge necessary and expedient;

SECTION 1 (CONTINUED)

2.1.8 Before the President actually exercises any of the powers or duties of office, he or she must take the following Oath or Affirmation: "I do solemnly swear (or affirm) that I will faithfully execute the office of President of the United States, and will to the best of my ability, preserve, protect, and defend the Constitution of the United States."

SECTION 2

2.2.1 The President will be Commander in Chief of the Army and Navy of the United States, and of the Militia of the separate States when they are called into the actual service of the United States. The President may require the written opinion of the Cabinet officers upon any subject relating to the duties of their respective offices. He or she will have Power to grant reprieves and pardons for offenses against the United States, except in cases of impeachment.

2.2.2a The President will have Power to make treaties with the advice and consent of the Senate. Two-thirds of the Senators present must agree. He or she must nominate and then appoint ambassadors, public officials, diplomats, Justices of the Supreme Court, and all other officers of the United States. This includes any appointments that are not provided for elsewhere in the Constitution, but are later established by Law. These appointments also require the advice and consent of the Senate.

2.2.2b However, Congress may give the President the Power to directly appoint certain lower-ranking officers. Congress may, by Law, give the same Power to the courts of Law or the heads of departments, as deemed proper.

2.2.3 The President will have Power to fill all vacancies that may happen during the recess of the Senate, by granting commissions that will expire at the end of the Senate's next session.

SECTION 3

2.3.1a The President must regularly give information to Congress concerning the State of the Union, and recommend for their consideration whatever measures he or she thinks are necessary and expedient.

SECTION. 3. (CONTINUED)

he may, on extraordinary Occasions, convene both Houses, or either of them, and in Case of Disagreement between them, with Respect to the Time of Adjournment, he may adjourn them to such Time as he shall think proper;

he shall receive Ambassadors and other public Ministers; he shall take Care that the Laws be faithfully executed, and shall Commission all the Officers of the United States.

SECTION. 4.

The President, Vice President and all civil Officers of the United States, shall be removed from Office on Impeachment for, and Conviction of, Treason, Bribery, or other high Crimes and Misdemeanors.

Article III.

SECTION. 1.

The judicial Power of the United States shall be vested in one supreme Court, and in such inferior Courts as the Congress may from time to time ordain and establish. The Judges, both of the supreme and inferior Courts, shall hold their Offices during good Behaviour, and shall, at stated Times, receive for their Services a Compensation, which shall not be diminished during their Continuance in Office.

SECTION. 2.

The judicial Power shall extend to all Cases, in Law and Equity, arising under this Constitution, the Laws of the United States, and Treaties made, or which shall be made, under their Authority;--to all Cases affecting Ambassadors, other public Ministers and Consuls;--to all Cases of admiralty and maritime Jurisdiction;--to Controversies to which the United States shall be a Party;--to Controversies between two or more States;-- between a State and Citizens of another State;--between Citizens of different States;--between Citizens of the same State claiming Lands under Grants of different States, and between a State, or the Citizens thereof, and foreign States, Citizens or Subjects. [Changed by the 11th Amendment.]

2.3.1b On extraordinary occasions, the President may convene one or both Houses of Congress. In cases when the two Houses disagree about when to adjourn, the President may adjourn them at the time he or she thinks is proper.

2.3.1c The President must receive ambassadors and other public officials. He or she must make sure that the Laws are faithfully carried out, and must commission all the officers of the United States.

SECTION 4
2.4.1 The President, Vice President, and all government officials of the United States must be removed from office if they are impeached for, and then convicted of, treason, bribery, or other political crimes or misdemeanors against the United States.

Article 3
SECTION 1
3.1.1 The judicial Power of the United States will be entrusted to one Supreme Court and in whatever lower courts Congress decides to create in the future. The Judges of all these courts may stay in office for as long as they demonstrate good behavior. They must be paid for their services on a regular basis, and their pay may not be decreased during their time in office.

SECTION 2
3.2.1 The judicial Power will encompass all civil and criminal cases that concern this Constitution, the Laws of the United States, and treaties made under their authority. The judicial Power will also encompass all cases affecting ambassadors, other public officers and diplomats, and all cases where the Laws of the oceans and seas apply. The judicial Power will also encompass all controversies in which the United States is one of the parties, all controversies between two or more States, between citizens of different States, and between citizens of the same State who are claiming lands under grants of different States.[51]

Section. 2. (continued)

In all Cases affecting Ambassadors, other public Ministers and Consuls, and those in which a State shall be Party, the supreme Court shall have original Jurisdiction. In all the other Cases before mentioned, the supreme Court shall have appellate Jurisdiction, both as to Law and Fact, with such Exceptions, and under such Regulations as the Congress shall make.

The Trial of all Crimes, except in Cases of Impeachment, shall be by Jury; and such Trial shall be held in the State where the said Crimes shall have been committed; but when not committed within any State, the Trial shall be at such Place or Places as the Congress may by Law have directed.

Section. 3.

Treason against the United States, shall consist only in levying War against them, or in adhering to their Enemies, giving them Aid and Comfort. No Person shall be convicted of Treason unless on the Testimony of two Witnesses to the same overt Act, or on Confession in open Court.

The Congress shall have Power to declare the Punishment of Treason, but no Attainder of Treason shall work Corruption of Blood, or Forfeiture except during the Life of the Person attainted.

Article. IV.

Section. 1.

Full Faith and Credit shall be given in each State to the public Acts, Records, and judicial Proceedings of every other State. And the Congress may by general Laws prescribe the Manner in which such Acts, Records and Proceedings shall be proved, and the Effect thereof.

Section. 2.

The Citizens of each State shall be entitled to all Privileges and Immunities of Citizens in the several States.

A Person charged in any State with Treason, Felony, or other Crime, who shall flee from Justice, and be found in another State, shall on Demand of

SECTION 2 (CONTINUED)

3.2.2 The Supreme Court will have primary authority over all cases that affect ambassadors, other public officials and diplomats, and those cases in which a State is involved. The Supreme Court will have authority in all the other cases previously mentioned if the cases are appealed to them. This authority will include both matters of Law and fact. There may be exceptions under regulations that Congress makes.

3.2.3 Trials for all crimes, except cases of impeachment, must be by jury; and these trials must be held in the State where the crimes were committed. If the crimes were not committed in any State, the trial will be held wherever Congress has decided by Law.

SECTION 3

3.3.1 Treason against the United States means making war against them, or joining with their enemies, or giving them assistance and support. A person may not be convicted of treason unless there is testimony from at least two witnesses to the same actual act, or unless the person confesses in a public courtroom.

3.3.2 Congress will have Power to declare the punishment for treason, but the penalty may not include confiscating a person's property after that person is executed.[52]

Article 4

SECTION 1

4.1.1 Each State must fully accept the public acts, records, and court actions of every other State. Congress may write general Laws[53] that describe how these acts, records, and court actions can be proven, and what effect they will have.

SECTION 2

4.2.1 The citizens of each State will be entitled to all the privileges and freedoms of citizens in the other States.

4.2.2 If a person is charged with treason, felony, or another crime in one State, then flees to another State and is found there, this fugitive must be

SECTION. 2. (CONTINUED)

the executive Authority of the State from which he fled, be delivered up, to be removed to the State having Jurisdiction of the Crime. <u>No Person held to Service or Labour in one State, under the Laws thereof, escaping into another, shall, in Consequence of any Law or Regulation therein, be discharged from such Service or Labour, but shall be delivered up on Claim of the Party to whom such Service or Labour may be due.</u>
[Changed by the 13th Amendment]

SECTION. 3.

New States may be admitted by the Congress into this Union; but no new State shall be formed or erected within the Jurisdiction of any other State; nor any State be formed by the Junction of two or more States, or Parts of States, without the Consent of the Legislatures of the States concerned as well as of the Congress.

The Congress shall have Power to dispose of and make all needful Rules and Regulations respecting the Territory or other Property belonging to the United States; and nothing in this Constitution shall be so construed as to Prejudice any Claims of the United States, or of any particular State.

SECTION. 4.

The United States shall guarantee to every State in this Union a Republican Form of Government, and shall protect each of them against Invasion; and on Application of the Legislature, or of the Executive (when the Legislature cannot be convened), against domestic Violence.

Article. V.

The Congress, whenever two thirds of both Houses shall deem it necessary, shall propose Amendments to this Constitution, or, on the Application of the Legislatures of two thirds of the several States, shall call a Convention for proposing Amendments,

which, in either Case, shall be valid to all Intents and Purposes, as Part of this Constitution, when ratified by the Legislatures of three fourths of the several States, or by Conventions in three fourths thereof, as the one or the other Mode of Ratification may be proposed by the Congress;

returned to the State he or she fled from, if the executive authority from that State demands it.

[**4.2.3** Made obsolete by the 13th Amendment][54]

SECTION 3

4.3.1 New States may be admitted into this Union by Congress. But no new State may be formed or created within the boundaries of any other State unless it is approved by Congress and the legislature of the State affected. And no new State may be formed by combining two or more States, or parts of those States, unless it is approved by Congress and the legislatures of the States affected.

4.3.2 Congress will have Power to sell or transfer the territory or other property belonging to the United States, and to make all necessary rules and regulations for them. But nothing in this Constitution may be interpreted in a way that it gives any State, or the United States, any preference concerning claims they may have.

SECTION 4

4.4.1 The United States will guarantee a republican form of government to every State in this Union, and will protect each of them from invasion. They will also be protected from domestic violence if the legislature of a State requests it. If the legislature cannot be convened, the Governor of that State may request it.

Article 5

5.1a Amendments to this Constitution may be proposed in two different ways. The first way is for Congress to propose them whenever two-thirds of both Houses decide it is necessary. The second way is for the legislatures of two-thirds of the States to request it, and then Congress must call a Convention for proposing Amendments.

5.1b Congress may propose one of two different ways for a proposed Amendment(s) to be ratified.[55] The first way is ratification by three-fourths of the State legislatures; the second is ratification by Conventions in three-fourths of the States. Any Amendment(s) that is approved will become an actual part(s) of the Constitution.

Provided that no Amendment which may be made prior to the Year One thousand eight hundred and eight shall in any Manner affect the first and fourth Clauses in the Ninth Section of the first Article; and that no State, without its Consent, shall be deprived of its equal Suffrage in the Senate.

Article. VI.

All Debts contracted and Engagements entered into, before the Adoption of this Constitution, shall be as valid against the United States under this Constitution, as under the Confederation.

This Constitution, and the Laws of the United States which shall be made in Pursuance thereof; and all Treaties made, or which shall be made, under the Authority of the United States, shall be the supreme Law of the Land; and the Judges in every State shall be bound thereby, any Thing in the Constitution or Laws of any State to the Contrary notwithstanding.

The Senators and Representatives before mentioned, and the Members of the several State Legislatures, and all executive and judicial Officers, both of the United States and of the several States, shall be bound by Oath or Affirmation, to support this Constitution; but no religious Test shall ever be required as a Qualification to any Office or public Trust under the United States.

Article. VII.

The Ratification of the Conventions of nine States, shall be sufficient for the Establishment of this Constitution between the States so ratifying the Same.

Done in Convention by the Unanimous Consent of the States present the Seventeenth Day of September in the Year of our Lord one thousand seven hundred and Eighty seven and of the Independence of the United States of America the Twelfth In witness whereof We have hereunto subscribed our Names,

G . Washington--President and deputy from Virginia

5.1c No Amendment may be made before the year 1808 that affects **C:1.9.1** or **C:1.9.4** of this Constitution in any way. No State may ever be deprived of equal representation in the Senate without its consent.

Article 6

6.1 All debts that have been incurred, and all agreements that have been made, before this Constitution becomes effective, will be just as binding upon the United States under this Constitution, as they were under the Confederation.[56]

6.2 This Constitution will be the supreme Law of the land, as are the Laws of the United States made in accordance with the Constitution, and all treaties made by the authority of the United States in the past and in the future. Judges in every State will be bound by this supreme Law, regardless of anything in any State Law or State Constitution.

6.3 All Senators and Representatives, and every member of every State legislature, and all executive and judicial officers of the United States and of every State, will be bound by Oath or Affirmation, to support this Constitution. But no religious test may ever be required as a qualification for any official position under the United States.

Article 7

7.1 Approval by the Conventions of nine States will be enough to establish this Constitution between the States that approve it.

7.2 This has been done in Convention, by the unanimous consent of the States who are present, on September 17, in the Year of our Lord 1787, which is also the twelfth year of the Independence of the United States of America. As witnesses of this we have signed our Names as follows:

George Washington—President and deputy from Virginia

Attest William Jackson Secretary

Delaware	Geo: Read, Gunning Bedford jun, John Dickinson, Richard Bassett Jaco: Broom
Maryland	James McHenry, Dan of St Thos. Jenifer, Danl Carroll
Virginia	John Blair, James Madison Jr.
North Carolina	Wm. Blount, Richd. Dobbs Spaight, Hu Williamson
South Carolina	J. Rutledge, Charles Cotesworth Pinckney, Charles Pinckney, Pierce Butler
Georgia	William Few, Abr Baldwin
New Hampshire	John Langdon, Nicholas Gilman
Massachusetts	Nathaniel Gorham, Rufus King
Connecticut	Wm. Saml. Johnson, Roger Sherman
New York	Alexander Hamilton
New Jersey	Wil: Livingston, David Brearley, Wm. Paterson, Jona: Dayton
Pennsylvania	B Franklin, Thomas Mifflin, Robt Morris, Geo. Clymer, Thos. FitzSimons, Jared Ingersoll, James Wilson, Gouv Morris

Attest William Jackson Secretary

Delaware: George Read, Gunning Bedford, Jr., John Dickinson, Richard Bassett, Jacob Broom

Maryland: James McHenry, Daniel of St. Thomas Jenifer, Daniel Carroll

Virginia: John Blair, James Madison Jr.

North Carolina: William Blount, Richard Dobbs Spaight, Hu Williamson

South Carolina: John Rutledge, Charles Cotesworth Pinckney, Charles Pinckney, Pierce Butler

Georgia: William Few, Abraham Baldwin

New Hampshire: John Langdon, Nicholas Gilman

Massachusetts: Nathaniel Gorham, Rufus King

Connecticut: William Samuel Johnson, Roger Sherman

New York: Alexander Hamilton

New Jersey: William Livingston, David Brearley, William Paterson, Jonathan Dayton

Pennsylvania: Benjamin Franklin, Thomas Mifflin, Robert Morris, George Clymer, Thomas FitzSimons, Jared Ingersoll, James Wilson, Gouvernor Morris

The Bill of Rights

Preamble

Congress of the United States
begun and held at the City of New-York, on Wednesday the fourth of
March, one thousand seven hundred and eighty nine.

THE Conventions of a number of the States, having at the time of
their adopting the Constitution, expressed a desire, in order to prevent
misconstruction or abuse of its powers, that further declaratory and
restrictive clauses should be added: And as extending the ground of public
confidence in the Government, will best ensure the beneficent ends of its
institution.

RESOLVED by the Senate and House of Representatives of the United States
of America, in Congress assembled, two thirds of both Houses concurring,
that the following Articles be proposed to the Legislatures of the several States,
as amendments to the Constitution of the United States, all, or any of which
Articles, when ratified by three fourths of the said Legislatures, to be valid to
all intents and purposes, as part of the said Constitution; viz.

ARTICLES in addition to, and Amendment of the Constitution of
the United States of America, proposed by Congress, and ratified by
the Legislatures of the several States, pursuant to the fifth Article of the
original Constitution.

[*Note: The following text is a transcription of the first ten Amendments to
the Constitution in their original form. These Amendments were ratified
December 15, 1791, and form what is known as the "Bill of Rights."*]

Amendment I

Congress shall make no law respecting an establishment of religion, or
prohibiting the free exercise thereof; or abridging the freedom of speech,
or of the press; or the right of the people peaceably to assemble, and to
petition the Government for a redress of grievances.

THE BILL OF RIGHTS[57]

Preamble

(The following is presented by the) Congress of the United States, which convened in New York City on Wednesday, March 4, 1789.

At the time that they adopted the Constitution, several of the State Conventions expressed a desire that further declarations and restrictions should be added in order to prevent misinterpretation or abuse of the Constitution's powers. Since doing so will increase the basis for public confidence in the Government, and is the best way to make sure that the results of establishing it are beneficial;

It is RESOLVED by the Senate and the House of Representatives of the United States of America, while assembled in Congress, and agreed to by two-thirds of both Houses, that the following Articles are to be proposed to the legislatures of the various States. Any of these Articles that are approved by three-fourths of the State legislatures will become Amendments to the Constitution, and will become valid as an actual part of the Constitution.

The following ARTICLES are in addition to, and Amendments of, the Constitution of the United States of America. They have been proposed by Congress and approved by the legislatures of the various States, as required by Article 5 of the original Constitution.

Amendment 1

Congress may not make any Law that establishes any religion, or interferes with any religious practice. Congress may not make any Law that diminishes the freedom of speech, or the freedom of the press, or the right of the people to assemble peacefully, or the right of the people to petition the Government to put things right if it has caused them harm.

Amendment II

A well regulated Militia, being necessary to the security of a free State, the right of the people to keep and bear Arms, shall not be infringed.

Amendment III

No Soldier shall, in time of peace be quartered in any house, without the consent of the Owner, nor in time of war, but in a manner to be prescribed by law.

Amendment IV

The right of the people to be secure in their persons, houses, papers, and effects, against unreasonable searches and seizures, shall not be violated, and no Warrants shall issue, but upon probable cause, supported by Oath or affirmation, and particularly describing the place to be searched, and the persons or things to be seized.

Amendment V

No person shall be held to answer for a capital, or otherwise infamous crime, unless on a presentment or indictment of a Grand Jury, except in cases arising in the land or naval forces, or in the Militia, when in actual service in time of War or public danger;

nor shall any person be subject for the same offence to be twice put in jeopardy of life or limb; nor shall be compelled in any criminal case to be a witness against himself, nor be deprived of life, liberty, or property, without due process of law; nor shall private property be taken for public use, without just compensation.

Amendment VI

In all criminal prosecutions, the accused shall enjoy the right to a speedy and public trial, by an impartial jury of the State and district wherein the crime shall have been committed, which district shall have been previously ascertained by law, and to be informed of the nature and cause of the accusation; to be confronted with the witnesses against him; to have compulsory process for obtaining witnesses in his favor, and to have the Assistance of Counsel for his defence.

Amendment 2

The people have the right to own and carry firearms,[58] and this right may not be violated because a well-equipped Militia[59] is necessary for a State to remain secure and free.

Amendment 3

Soldiers may not be housed in private homes in peacetime unless the owner gives his consent. Soldiers may only be housed in private homes in wartime in a way that will be described by Law.

Amendment 4

The people have the right to be protected from unreasonable searches and seizures, and this right may not be violated. This protection includes their persons, houses, papers, and belongings. No warrant may be issued unless it is reasonably believed that a crime was most likely committed.[60] This belief must be supported by a sworn statement[61] and the warrant must specifically describe the place to be searched, and the persons or things to be seized.

Amendment 5

5a No one may be tried for a crime that might be punishable by death, or for any other terrible crime, unless he or she is first indicted by a Grand Jury. The exceptions are cases involving the Army or Navy, and cases involving the Militia when they are actually serving during time of war or public danger.

5b No one may be tried twice for the same crime in cases where the resulting penalty might be capital punishment.[62] No one may be forced to testify against himself or herself in any criminal case. No one may be deprived of life, liberty, or property without his or her legal rights being processed under the proper operation of Law. No private property may be taken for public use without fair compensation.

Amendment 6

In all criminal cases, the accused person has the right to a speedy and public trial by an impartial jury from the State and district where the crime was committed. This district must have been previously determined by Law. The accused person also has the right to be informed of the exact nature of and grounds of the accusation, to confront the witnesses against him or her, to call witnesses in his or her favor to testify, and to have the assistance of a lawyer for his or her defense.

Amendment VII

In Suits at common law, where the value in controversy shall exceed twenty dollars, the right of trial by jury shall be preserved, and no fact tried by a jury, shall be otherwise re-examined in any Court of the United States, than according to the rules of the common law.

Amendment VIII

Excessive bail shall not be required, nor excessive fines imposed, nor cruel and unusual punishments inflicted.

Amendment IX

The enumeration in the Constitution, of certain rights, shall not be construed to deny or disparage others retained by the people.

Amendment X

The powers not delegated to the United States by the Constitution, nor prohibited by it to the States, are reserved to the States respectively, or to the people.

Amendments XI–XXVII

AMENDMENT XI
Passed by Congress March 4, 1794. Ratified February 7, 1795.
[Note: Article III, section II of the Constitution was modified by 11th Amendment.]
The Judicial power of the United States shall not be construed to extend to any suit in law or equity, commenced or prosecuted against one of the United States by Citizens of another State, or by Citizens or Subjects of any Foreign State.

AMENDMENT XII
Passed by Congress December 9, 1803. Ratified June 15, 1804.
*[**Note:** A portion of Article II, section I of the Constitution was superseded by the 12th Amendment.]*
The Electors shall meet in their respective states and vote by ballot for President and Vice-President, one of whom, at least, shall not be an inhabitant of the same state with themselves;

Amendment 7

In lawsuits under common law,[63] where the disputed amount is more than twenty dollars, the right of trial by jury will be preserved. No fact that has been tried by a jury may be reexamined in any court of the United States, except according to the rules of common law.

Amendment 8

Excessive bail cannot be required. Excessive fines cannot be imposed. Cruel and unusual punishments cannot be inflicted.

Amendment 9

The fact that certain rights of the people are listed in the Constitution does not mean that their other rights may be denied or disrespected.[64]

Amendment 10

The Powers that are not delegated to the United States by the Constitution are retained by the separate States or by the people. There are exceptions for certain powers that the Constitution prohibits to the States.[65]

AMENDMENTS 11–27

Amendment 11[66]

The judicial Power of the United States will no longer include any kind of suit that is brought against one of the United States by citizens of any other State, or by citizens or subjects of any foreign country.

Amendment 12[67]

12a The electors must meet in their respective States, and vote by ballot for President and Vice President. They may not vote for a President and a Vice President who are both from the same State as the electors.

they shall name in their ballots the person voted for as President, and in distinct ballots the person voted for as Vice-President, and they shall make distinct lists of all persons voted for as President, and of all persons voted for as Vice-President, and of the number of votes for each, which lists they shall sign and certify, and transmit sealed to the seat of the government of the United States, directed to the President of the Senate;

-- the President of the Senate shall, in the presence of the Senate and House of Representatives, open all the certificates and the votes shall then be counted; -- The person having the greatest number of votes for President, shall be the President, if such number be a majority of the whole number of Electors appointed;

and if no person have such majority, then from the persons having the highest numbers not exceeding three on the list of those voted for as President, the House of Representatives shall choose immediately, by ballot, the President. But in choosing the President, the votes shall be taken by states, the representation from each state having one vote; a quorum for this purpose shall consist of a member or members from two-thirds of the states, and a majority of all the states shall be necessary to a choice.

And if the House of Representatives shall not choose a President whenever the right of choice shall devolve upon them, before the fourth day of March next following, then the Vice-President shall act as President, as in case of the death or other constitutional disability of the President. *[Note: Superseded by Section 3 of the 20th Amendment.]*

[See Section 3 of the 20th Amendment]

The person having the greatest number of votes as Vice-President, shall be the Vice-President, if such number be a majority of the whole number of Electors appointed, and if no person have a majority, then from the two

12b They must name in one set of ballots the person they voted for as President, and in a different set of ballots the person they voted for as Vice President. They must make separate lists of all the persons they voted for as President, and of all persons they voted for as Vice President, and the number of votes for each. They must sign these lists, and certify that they are correct, and send them sealed to the President of the Senate.

12c The President of the Senate must open all the certificates in the presence of the Senate and House of Representatives, and the votes must then be counted. The person receiving the greatest number of votes for President will become the President, as long as he or she receives a majority of the total number of electors.

12d If no person receives a majority, then the House of Representatives must immediately elect the President by ballot. They must choose him or her from the three persons with the highest numbers of votes. In choosing the President, the votes must be taken by States, and each State will have one vote. A quorum for this purpose will consist of at least one member from two-thirds of the States, and a majority of all the States will be necessary for the election to be final.

12e[68] If the President elect dies before the beginning of his or her term (noon, January 20), then the Vice President-elect will become President. If a President has not been chosen before the beginning of his or her term, or if the President-elect does not qualify, then the Vice President-elect will act as President until a qualified President is chosen. [From **A:20.3.1**]

12f If neither a President elect nor a Vice President-elect qualifies, Congress may provide for this eventuality by Law. Then this law will determine who will act as President, or the way in which the Acting President will be selected. This person will act as President until a qualified President or Vice President is chosen. [From **A:20.3.2**]

12g The person receiving the greatest number of votes for Vice President will become the Vice President, as long as he or she receives a majority of the total number of electors. If no person receives a majority, then the Senate must choose the Vice President from the two persons with the highest numbers

AMENDMENT XII (CONTINUED)

highest numbers on the list, the Senate shall choose the Vice-President; a quorum for the purpose shall consist of two-thirds of the whole number of Senators, and a majority of the whole number shall be necessary to a choice. But no person constitutionally ineligible to the office of President shall be eligible to that of Vice-President of the United States.

AMENDMENT XIII

Passed by Congress January 31, 1865. Ratified December 6, 1865.

*[**Note:** A portion of Article IV, section 2 of the Constitution was superseded by the 13th Amendment.]*

SECTION 1.

Neither slavery nor involuntary servitude, except as a punishment for crime whereof the party shall have been duly convicted, shall exist within the United States, or any place subject to their jurisdiction.

SECTION 2.

Congress shall have power to enforce this article by appropriate legislation.

AMENDMENT XIV

Passed by Congress June 13, 1866. Ratified July 9, 1868.

*[**Note:** Article I, section 2, of the Constitution was modified by section 2 of the 14th Amendment.]*

SECTION 1.

All persons born or naturalized in the United States, and subject to the jurisdiction thereof, are citizens of the United States and of the State wherein they reside. No State shall make or enforce any law which shall abridge the privileges or immunities of citizens of the United States; nor shall any State deprive any person of life, liberty, or property, without due process of law; nor deny to any person within its jurisdiction the equal protection of the laws.

SECTION 2.

Representatives shall be apportioned among the several States according to their respective numbers, counting the whole number of persons in each State, excluding Indians not taxed. But when the right to vote at any election for the choice of electors for President and Vice-President of the United of votes. A quorum for this purpose will consist of two-thirds of the total number of Senators, and a majority of the total number will be necessary for the election to be final. If a person is not eligible, under the Constitution, to be President of the United States, that person will not be eligible to be Vice President either.

Amendment 13[69]

SECTION 1
Slavery and all other forms of involuntary servitude are forbidden within the United States, and all places under their authority, unless it is punishment for a crime for which the person has been properly convicted.

SECTION 2
Congress will have power to enforce this Amendment by appropriate Laws.

Amendment 14[70]

SECTION 1
All people who are born or naturalized in the United States, and subject to their authority, are citizens of the United States and of the State they live in. No State may make or enforce any Law that diminishes the privileges or freedoms of citizens of the United States. No State may take away any person's life, liberty, or property without proper operation of Law. No State may deny any person under its authority the equal protection of the Laws.

SECTION 2
The number of Representatives that each State has will be based upon the population of each State. For these purposes the population will count everybody except tax-exempt American Indians [who live and work on reservations]. The right to vote may not be denied to any citizen in any State who is at least eighteen years old.[71] This includes the right to vote

AMENDMENT XIV/Section 2. (continued)

States, Representatives in Congress, the Executive and Judicial officers of a State, or the members of the Legislature thereof, is denied to any of <u>the male inhabitants</u> of such State, being <u>twenty-one years of age</u>, and citizens of the United States, or in any way abridged, except for participation in rebellion, or other crime, the basis of representation therein shall be reduced in the proportion which the number of such <u>male citizens</u> shall bear to the whole number of <u>male citizens</u> <u>twenty-one years of age</u> in such State.

Section 3.

No person shall be a Senator or Representative in Congress, or elector of President and Vice-President, or hold any office, civil or military, under the United States, or under any State, who, having previously taken an oath, as a member of Congress, or as an officer of the United States, or as a member of any State legislature, or as an executive or judicial officer of any State, to support the Constitution of the United States, shall have engaged in insurrection or rebellion against the same, or given aid or comfort to the enemies thereof. But Congress may by a vote of two-thirds of each House, remove such disability.

Section 4.

The validity of the public debt of the United States, authorized by law, including debts incurred for payment of pensions and bounties for services in suppressing insurrection or rebellion, shall not be questioned. But neither the United States nor any State shall assume or pay any debt or obligation incurred in aid of insurrection or rebellion against the United States, or any claim for the loss or emancipation of any slave; but all such debts, obligations and claims shall be held illegal and void.

Section 5.

The Congress shall have the power to enforce, by appropriate legislation, the provisions of this article.

AMENDMENT XV

Passed by Congress February 26, 1869. Ratified February 3, 1870.

Section 1.

The right of citizens of the United States to vote shall not be denied or for President and Vice President of the United States,[72] Representatives in Congress, and the Governor, Judges, and Legislators of that State. If any State prevents or hinders any eligible citizen from voting, unless he or she participated in rebellion or other crime, the number of Representatives that State is entitled to will be reduced in proportion.

SECTION 3

Certain people are disqualified from being Senators or Representatives in Congress, or from being electors of the President and Vice President, or from holding any official position under the United States or under any State.[73] If an individual was ever a member of Congress, or a member of a State legislature, or an officer of the United States, or an official in any State, and took an oath to support the Constitution of the United States and then either participated in revolution or rebellion against the Constitution or gave assistance or support to its enemies, then they are disqualified. However, Congress may make exceptions in such cases by a two-thirds vote of each House.

SECTION 4

The public debt of the United States is valid and may not be questioned if the debt was authorized by law. These debts include payment of pensions and rewards for services used in suppressing revolution or rebellion. But, neither the United States nor any State may assume or pay any debt or obligation incurred as part of any revolution or rebellion against the United States. They may not pay any claim for the loss or freeing of any slave. All such debts, obligations and claims will be regarded as illegal and void.[74]

SECTION 5

Congress will have the Power to enforce the provisions of this Amendment by appropriate Laws.

Amendment 15[75]

SECTION 1

The right of citizens of the United States to vote shall not be denied or

AMENDMENT XV/Section 1. (continued)

abridged by the United States or by any State on account of race, color, or previous condition of servitude —

Section 2.

The Congress shall have the power to enforce this article by appropriate legislation.

AMENDMENT XVI
Passed by Congress July 2, 1909. Ratified February 3, 1913.

[Note: Article I, section 9, of the Constitution was modified by Amendment 16.]
The Congress shall have power to lay and collect taxes on incomes, from whatever source derived, without apportionment among the several States, and without regard to any census or enumeration.

AMENDMENT XVII
Passed by Congress May 13, 1912. Ratified April 8, 1913.

[Note: Article I, section 3, of the Constitution was modified by the 17th Amendment.]
The Senate of the United States shall be composed of two Senators from each State, elected by the people thereof, for six years; and each Senator shall have one vote. The electors in each State shall have the qualifications requisite for electors of the most numerous branch of the State legislatures.

When vacancies happen in the representation of any State in the Senate, the executive authority of such State shall issue writs of election to fill such vacancies: *Provided,* That the legislature of any State may empower the executive thereof to make temporary appointments until the people fill the vacancies by election as the legislature may direct.

This amendment shall not be so construed as to affect the election or term of any Senator chosen before it becomes valid as part of the Constitution.

diminished by the United States or by any State because of their race or color, or because they were previously a slave.

SECTION 2
Congress will have the Power to enforce this Amendment by appropriate Laws.

Amendment 16[76]

Congress will have the Power to assess and collect taxes on income from all sources. These taxes will not be based on the census, or divided proportionately between the States.

Amendment 17[77]

17a The Senate of the United States will consist of two Senators from each State, elected by the people of that State, for six years; and each Senator will have one vote. Each State has a standard it uses to decide who is allowed to vote for its own State legislature. This same standard must be used to determine who is allowed to vote for members of the Senate.

17b When any Senator does not finish his or her term, the Governor from his or her State must set a Special Election to fill the remainder of that term. However, the legislature of that State may give the Governor Power to make a temporary appointment that will only last until the position is filled by the Special Election.

17c This Amendment may not be interpreted in a way that affects the election or term of any Senator who has already been elected when this Amendment becomes part of the Constitution.

AMENDMENT XVIII

Passed by Congress December 18, 1917. Ratified January 16, 1919. Repealed by Amendment 21.

SECTION 1.

After one year from the ratification of this article the manufacture, sale, or transportation of intoxicating liquors within, the importation thereof into, or the exportation thereof from the United States and all territory subject to the jurisdiction thereof for beverage purposes is hereby prohibited.

SECTION 2.

The Congress and the several States shall have concurrent power to enforce this article by appropriate legislation.

SECTION 3.

This article shall be inoperative unless it shall have been ratified as an amendment to the Constitution by the legislatures of the several States, as provided in the Constitution, within seven years from the date of the submission hereof to the States by the Congress.

AMENDMENT XIX

Passed by Congress June 4, 1919. Ratified August 18, 1920.

The right of citizens of the United States to vote shall not be denied or abridged by the United States or by any State on account of sex.

Congress shall have power to enforce this article by appropriate legislation.

AMENDMENT XX

Passed by Congress March 2, 1932. Ratified January 23, 1933.

*[**Note:** Article I, section 4, of the Constitution was modified by section 2 of this amendment. In addition, a portion of the 12th amendment was superseded by section 3.]*

SECTION 1.

The terms of the President and the Vice President shall end at noon on the 20th day of January, and the terms of Senators and Representatives at noon on the 3d day of January, of the years in which such terms would have ended if this article had not been ratified; and the terms of their successors shall then begin.

Amendment 18

SECTION 1
One year after this Amendment receives final approval, it will be illegal to manufacture, sell, or transport alcoholic beverages within the United States and U.S. Territories. It will also be illegal to import or export alcoholic beverages into, or out of, the United States and U.S. territories. *[Note: Replaced by the 21st Amendment]*[78]

SECTION 2
Congress and the separate States will all have the Power to make Laws that enforce this Amendment.

SECTION 3
This Amendment will not go into effect unless it is approved by the legislatures of the various States, as described in the Constitution. The final approval process must also be completed within seven years from the date Congress sends it to the States.

Amendment 19[79]

19a The right of citizens of the United States to vote shall not be denied or diminished by the United States or by any State because of gender.

19b Congress will have the Power to enforce this Amendment by appropriate Laws.

Amendment 20

SECTION 1[80]
The terms of the President and the Vice President will end at noon on January 20. The terms of Senators and Representatives will end at noon on January 3. The terms of their successors will then begin. The years in which these various terms end, and others begin, is not changed by this Amendment.

AMENDMENT XX (CONTINUED)

SECTION 2.

The Congress shall assemble at least once in every year, and such meeting shall begin at noon on the 3d day of January, unless they shall by law appoint a different day.

SECTION 3.

If, at the time fixed for the beginning of the term of the President, the President elect shall have died, the Vice President elect shall become President. If a President shall not have been chosen before the time fixed for the beginning of his term, or if the President elect shall have failed to qualify, then the Vice President elect shall act as President until a President shall have qualified;

and the Congress may by law provide for the case wherein neither a President elect nor a Vice President shall have qualified, declaring who shall then act as President, or the manner in which one who is to act shall be selected, and such person shall act accordingly until a President or Vice President shall have qualified.

SECTION 4.

The Congress may by law provide for the case of the death of any of the persons from whom the House of Representatives may choose a President whenever the right of choice shall have devolved upon them, and for the case of the death of any of the persons from whom the Senate may choose a Vice President whenever the right of choice shall have devolved upon them.

SECTION 5.

Sections 1 and 2 shall take effect on the 15th day of October following the ratification of this article.

SECTION 6.

This article shall be inoperative unless it shall have been ratified as an amendment to the Constitution by the legislatures of three-fourths of the several States within seven years from the date of its submission.

AMENDMENT 20 (CONTINUED)
SECTION 2[81]
Congress must meet at least once in every year, and the meeting will begin at noon on January 3, unless the date is changed by Law.

SECTION 3[82]
20.3.a If the President-elect dies before the beginning of his or her term (noon, January 20), then the Vice President–elect will become President. If a President has not been chosen before the beginning of his or her term, or if the President-elect does not qualify, then the Vice President–elect will act as President until a qualified President is chosen.

20.3.b In case neither a President-elect nor a Vice President–elect qualifies, Congress may provide for this by Law. Then this Law will determine who will act as President, or the way in which the Acting President will be selected. This person will act as President until a qualified President or Vice President is chosen.

SECTION 4
The right to choose the President may become the responsibility of the House of Representatives (see **A:12d**). The right to choose the Vice President may become the responsibility of the Senate (see **A:12g**). In either case, if either this presidential or vice presidential candidate dies, Congress may write a Law to determine the course for choosing a successor(s).

SECTION 5
Sections 1 and 2 shall take effect on the October 15 following the final approval of this Amendment.

SECTION 6
This Amendment will not go into effect unless it is approved by the legislatures of three-fourths of the States. The final approval process must also be completed within seven years from the date Congress sends it to the States.

AMENDMENT XXI

Passed by Congress February 20, 1933. Ratified December 5, 1933.

SECTION 1.

The eighteenth article of amendment to the Constitution of the United States is hereby repealed.

SECTION 2.

The transportation or importation into any State, Territory, or Possession of the United States for delivery or use therein of intoxicating liquors, in violation of the laws thereof, is hereby prohibited.

SECTION 3.

This article shall be inoperative unless it shall have been ratified as an amendment to the Constitution by conventions in the several States, as provided in the Constitution, within seven years from the date of the submission hereof to the States by the Congress.

AMENDMENT XXII

Passed by Congress March 21, 1947. Ratified February 27, 1951.

SECTION 1.

No person shall be elected to the office of the President more than twice, and no person who has held the office of President, or acted as President, for more than two years of a term to which some other person was elected President shall be elected to the office of President more than once. But this Article shall not apply to any person holding the office of President when this Article was proposed by Congress, and shall not prevent any person who may be holding the office of President, or acting as President, during the term within which this Article becomes operative from holding the office of President or acting as President during the remainder of such term.

SECTION 2.

This article shall be inoperative unless it shall have been ratified as an amendment to the Constitution by the legislatures of three-fourths of the several States within seven years from the date of its submission to the States by the Congress.

Amendment 21

SECTION 1
This Amendment repeals (cancels out) the 18th Amendment of the Constitution.

SECTION 2
Alcoholic beverages may not be transported or imported into any State, Territory, or Possession of the United States if it violates their laws, and if these beverages are going to be delivered or consumed there.

SECTION 3
This Amendment will not go into effect unless it is approved by the legislatures of the various States, as described in the Constitution. The final approval process must also be completed within seven years from the date Congress sends it to the States.

Amendment 22[83]

SECTION 1
No person may be elected to the office of President more than twice. If a person has already served as President or Acting President for more than two years of someone else's term, he or she may only be elected once. This Amendment will not apply to the person who is President or Acting President when this Amendment was proposed by Congress. If this Amendment is approved and becomes effective, it will not prevent the person who is President or Acting President at that time from finishing his or her term.

SECTION 2
This Amendment will not go into effect unless it is approved by the legislatures of three-fourths of the States. The final approval process must also be completed within seven years from the date Congress sends it to the States.

AMENDMENT XXIII

Passed by Congress June 16, 1960. Ratified March 29, 1961.

SECTION 1.

The District constituting the seat of Government of the United States shall appoint in such manner as Congress may direct:

A number of electors of President and Vice President equal to the whole number of Senators and Representatives in Congress to which the District would be entitled if it were a State, but in no event more than the least populous State; they shall be in addition to those appointed by the States, but they shall be considered, for the purposes of the election of President and Vice President, to be electors appointed by a State; and they shall meet in the District and perform such duties as provided by the twelfth article of amendment.

SECTION 2.

The Congress shall have power to enforce this article by appropriate legislation.

AMENDMENT XXIV

Passed by Congress August 27, 1962. Ratified January 23, 1964.

SECTION 1.

The right of citizens of the United States to vote in any primary or other election for President or Vice President, for electors for President or Vice President, or for Senator or Representative in Congress, shall not be denied or abridged by the United States or any State by reason of failure to pay poll tax or other tax.

SECTION 2.

The Congress shall have power to enforce this article by appropriate legislation.

AMENDMENT XXV

Passed by Congress July 6, 1965. Ratificd February 10, 1967.

*[**Note:** Article II, section 1, of the Constitution was affected by the 25th amendment.]*

SECTION 1.

In case of the removal of the President from office or of his death or resignation, the Vice President shall become President.

Amendment 23[84]

SECTION 1

Washington, D.C.[85] may appoint electors for President and Vice President in the way that Congress decides. The number of electors will be calculated as if this District was the State with the least population. These electors will be in addition to the ones appointed by the States, but they shall be treated the same as if they were appointed by a State for this purpose. They shall meet in the District and perform the same duties that are required of States by the 12th Amendment.

SECTION 2

Congress will have the Power to enforce this Amendment by appropriate Laws.

Amendment 24[86]

SECTION 1

The right of citizens of the United States to vote shall not be denied or diminished by the United States or by any State for failure to pay a poll tax or other tax. This right includes voting in primary elections and other elections. It includes voting for President and Vice President,[87] and voting for Senators and Representatives in Congress.

SECTION 2

Congress will have the Power to enforce this Amendment by appropriate Laws.

Amendment 25[88]

SECTION 1

In case of the removal of the President from office, or of his or her death or resignation, the Vice President will become President.

AMENDMENT XXV (continued)

Section 2.

Whenever there is a vacancy in the office of the Vice President, the President shall nominate a Vice President who shall take office upon confirmation by a majority vote of both Houses of Congress.

Section 3.

Whenever the President transmits to the President pro tempore of the Senate and the Speaker of the House of Representatives his written declaration that he is unable to discharge the powers and duties of his office, and until he transmits to them a written declaration to the contrary, such powers and duties shall be discharged by the Vice President as Acting President.

Section 4.

Whenever the Vice President and a majority of either the principal officers of the executive departments or of such other body as Congress may by law provide, transmit to the President pro tempore of the Senate and the Speaker of the House of Representatives their written declaration that the President is unable to discharge the powers and duties of his office, the Vice President shall immediately assume the powers and duties of the office as Acting President.

Thereafter, when the President transmits to the President pro tempore of the Senate and the Speaker of the House of Representatives his written declaration that no inability exists, he shall resume the powers and duties of his office unless the Vice President and a majority of either the principal officers of the executive department or of such other body as Congress may by law provide, transmit within four days to the President pro tempore of the Senate and the Speaker of the House of Representatives their written declaration that the President is unable to discharge the powers and duties of his office.

Thereupon Congress shall decide the issue, assembling within forty-eight hours for that purpose if not in session. If the Congress, within twenty-one days after receipt of the latter written declaration, or, if Congress is not in session, within twenty-one days after Congress is required to assemble, determines by two-thirds vote of both Houses that the President is unable to

AMENDMENT 25 (CONTINUED)
SECTION 2
Whenever there is a vacancy in the office of the Vice President, the President must nominate a new Vice President. He or she will take office upon confirmation by a majority vote of both Houses of Congress.

SECTION 3
Whenever the President believes that he or she is unable to carry out the powers and duties of office, he or she may send written declaration to the temporary President of the Senate and to the Speaker of the House of Representatives. Until the President sends them a written declaration that he or she has become able again, these powers and duties must be discharged by the Vice President as Acting President.

SECTION 4
25.4.1 Whenever the Vice President and a majority of the Cabinet officers[89] or some other group Congress designates by Law agree that the President is unable to discharge the powers and duties of office, they may send their written declaration to the temporary President of the Senate and the Speaker of the House of Representatives. Then the Vice President must immediately assume the powers and duties as Acting President.

25.4.2a If, in response, the President believes that no inability exists, he or she must send written declaration to the temporary President of the Senate and to the Speaker of the House of Representatives. The President will resume the powers and duties of office unless the Vice President and a majority of the Cabinet officers oppose him or her. If they do, they must send their written declaration within four days to the temporary President of the Senate and to the Speaker of the House of Representatives reasserting that the President is unable to discharge the powers and duties of office.

25.4.2b At this point, Congress must decide the issue. They must meet within forty-eight hours for this purpose if they are not already in session. Congress must make a determination within twenty-one days of receiving the most recent declaration (or twenty-three days if they were not in session). If Congress determines that the President is unable to discharge the powers and duties of office, then the Vice President will continue as

AMENDMENT XXV (CONTINUED)

discharge the powers and duties of his office, the Vice President shall continue to discharge the same as Acting President; otherwise, the President shall resume the powers and duties of his office.

AMENDMENT XXVI

Passed by Congress March 23, 1971. Ratified July 1, 1971.

*[**Note:** Amendment 14, section 2, of the Constitution was modified by section 1 of the 26th amendment.]*

SECTION 1.

The right of citizens of the United States, who are eighteen years of age or older, to vote shall not be denied or abridged by the United States or by any State on account of age.

SECTION 2.

The Congress shall have power to enforce this article by appropriate legislation.

AMENDMENT XXVII

Originally proposed Sept. 25, 1789. Ratified May 7, 1992.

No law, varying the compensation for the services of the Senators and Representatives, shall take effect, until an election of representatives shall have intervened.

Acting President. This must be done by a two-thirds vote of both Houses. Otherwise, the President will resume the powers and duties of his or her office.

Amendment 26[90]

SECTION 1
The right of citizens of the United States to vote shall not be denied or diminished by the United States, or by any State, because of age, as long as they are eighteen years of age or older.

SECTION 2
Congress will have the Power to enforce this Amendment by appropriate Laws.

Amendment 27[91]
No Law that changes the pay of Senators and Representatives will take effect until after the next election of Representatives has taken place.

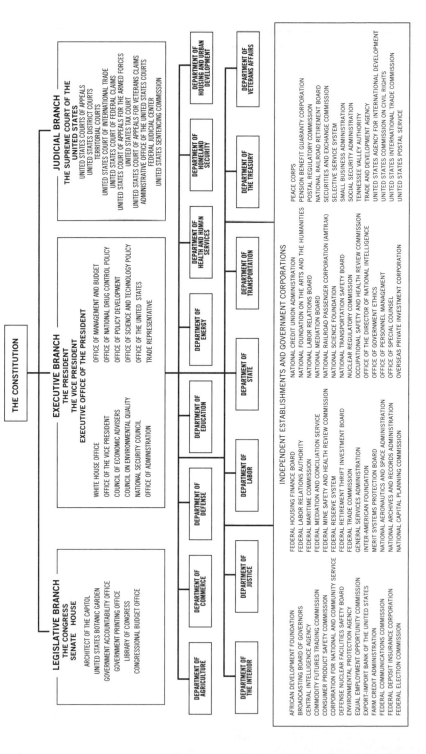

BRANCHES OF U.S. GOVERNMENT

THE CONSTITUTION

LEGISLATIVE BRANCH
THE CONGRESS
SENATE   HOUSE

ARCHITECT OF THE CAPITOL
UNITED STATES BOTANIC GARDEN
GOVERNMENT ACCOUNTABILITY OFFICE
GOVERNMENT PRINTING OFFICE
LIBRARY OF CONGRESS
CONGRESSIONAL BUDGET OFFICE

EXECUTIVE BRANCH
THE PRESIDENT
THE VICE PRESIDENT
EXECUTIVE OFFICE OF THE PRESIDENT

WHITE HOUSE OFFICE
OFFICE OF THE VICE PRESIDENT
COUNCIL OF ECONOMIC ADVISERS
COUNCIL ON ENVIRONMENTAL QUALITY
NATIONAL SECURITY COUNCIL
OFFICE OF ADMINISTRATION

OFFICE OF MANAGEMENT AND BUDGET
OFFICE OF NATIONAL DRUG CONTROL POLICY
OFFICE OF POLICY DEVELOPMENT
OFFICE OF SCIENCE AND TECHNOLOGY POLICY
OFFICE OF THE UNITED STATES
TRADE REPRESENTATIVE

JUDICIAL BRANCH
THE SUPREME COURT OF THE UNITED STATES

UNITED STATES COURTS OF APPEALS
UNITED STATES DISTRICT COURTS
TERRITORIAL COURTS
UNITED STATES COURT OF INTERNATIONAL TRADE
UNITED STATES COURT OF FEDERAL CLAIMS
UNITED STATES COURT OF APPEALS FOR THE ARMED FORCES
UNITED STATES TAX COURT
UNITED STATES COURT OF APPEALS FOR VETERANS CLAIMS
ADMINISTRATIVE OFFICE OF THE UNITED STATES COURTS
FEDERAL JUDICIAL CENTER
UNITED STATES SENTENCING COMMISSION

DEPARTMENT OF AGRICULTURE
DEPARTMENT OF COMMERCE
DEPARTMENT OF EDUCATION
DEPARTMENT OF ENERGY
DEPARTMENT OF HEALTH AND HUMAN SERVICES
DEPARTMENT OF HOUSING AND URBAN DEVELOPMENT

DEPARTMENT OF THE INTERIOR
DEPARTMENT OF JUSTICE
DEPARTMENT OF LABOR
DEPARTMENT OF STATE
DEPARTMENT OF TRANSPORTATION
DEPARTMENT OF THE TREASURY
DEPARTMENT OF VETERANS AFFAIRS

DEPARTMENT OF DEFENSE
DEPARTMENT OF HOMELAND SECURITY

INDEPENDENT ESTABLISHMENTS AND GOVERNMENT CORPORATIONS

AFRICAN DEVELOPMENT FOUNDATION
BROADCASTING BOARD OF GOVERNORS
CENTRAL INTELLIGENCE AGENCY
COMMODITY FUTURES TRADING COMMISSION
CONSUMER PRODUCT SAFETY COMMISSION
CORPORATION FOR NATIONAL AND COMMUNITY SERVICE
DEFENSE NUCLEAR FACILITIES SAFETY BOARD
ENVIRONMENTAL PROTECTION AGENCY
EQUAL EMPLOYMENT OPPORTUNITY COMMISSION
EXPORT-IMPORT BANK OF THE UNITED STATES
FARM CREDIT ADMINISTRATION
FEDERAL COMMUNICATIONS COMMISSION
FEDERAL DEPOSIT INSURANCE CORPORATION
FEDERAL ELECTION COMMISSION

FEDERAL HOUSING FINANCE BOARD
FEDERAL LABOR RELATIONS AUTHORITY
FEDERAL MARITIME COMMISSION
FEDERAL MEDIATION AND CONCILIATION SERVICE
FEDERAL MINE SAFETY AND HEALTH REVIEW COMMISSION
FEDERAL RESERVE SYSTEM
FEDERAL RETIREMENT THRIFT INVESTMENT BOARD
FEDERAL TRADE COMMISSION
GENERAL SERVICES ADMINISTRATION
INTER-AMERICAN FOUNDATION
MERIT SYSTEMS PROTECTION BOARD
NATIONAL AERONAUTICS AND SPACE ADMINISTRATION
NATIONAL ARCHIVES AND RECORDS ADMINISTRATION
NATIONAL CAPITAL PLANNING COMMISSION

NATIONAL CREDIT UNION ADMINISTRATION
NATIONAL FOUNDATION ON THE ARTS AND THE HUMANITIES
NATIONAL LABOR RELATIONS BOARD
NATIONAL MEDIATION BOARD
NATIONAL RAILROAD PASSENGER CORPORATION (AMTRAK)
NATIONAL SCIENCE FOUNDATION
NATIONAL TRANSPORTATION SAFETY BOARD
NUCLEAR REGULATORY COMMISSION
OCCUPATIONAL SAFETY AND HEALTH REVIEW COMMISSION
OFFICE OF THE DIRECTOR OF NATIONAL INTELLIGENCE
OFFICE OF GOVERNMENT ETHICS
OFFICE OF PERSONNEL MANAGEMENT
OFFICE OF SPECIAL COUNSEL
OVERSEAS PRIVATE INVESTMENT CORPORATION

PEACE CORPS
PENSION BENEFIT GUARANTY CORPORATION
POSTAL REGULATORY COMMISSION
NATIONAL RAILROAD RETIREMENT BOARD
SECURITIES AND EXCHANGE COMMISSION
SELECTIVE SERVICE SYSTEM
SMALL BUSINESS ADMINISTRATION
SOCIAL SECURITY ADMINISTRATION
TENNESSEE VALLEY AUTHORITY
TRADE AND DEVELOPMENT AGENCY
UNITED STATES AGENCY FOR INTERNATIONAL DEVELOPMENT
UNITED STATES COMMISSION ON CIVIL RIGHTS
UNITED STATES INTERNATIONAL TRADE COMMISSION
UNITED STATES POSTAL SERVICE

INTRODUCTION ENDNOTES

1 A quote made by Winston Churchill in Perth, Scotland, on May 28, 1948. See: http://www.winstonchurchill.org/component/content/article/16-quotes/474.

2 George Washington, Farewell Address, published in the *American Daily Advertiser*, September 19, 1796. See: http://ourdocuments.gov/doc.php?flash=true&doc=15.

3 George Orwell, "Politics and the English Language," *Horizon* 13, issue 76 (1946).

4 Ronald Reagan, "A Time for Choosing," known as "The Speech," October 27, 1964, presented during the 1964 presidential campaign on behalf of Barry Goldwater. See: http://www.reagan.utexas.edu/archives/reference /timechoosing.html.

5 Paul Prentice, from numerous speeches in 2011, and e-mail of November 13, 2011.

6 Howard Kaloogian, in speeches made August and September 2011 at Tea Party Express V.

7 Thomas Jefferson, Kentucky Resolution, November 16, 1798. See: http://memory. loc.gov/cgi-bin/ampage?collId=lled&fileName=004/lled004.db&recNum=554.

8 James Madison, "Outline Notes," September 1829. See: http://www.loc.gov/loc/walls/madison.html.

9 Woodrow Wilson, *Congressional Government: A Study in American Politics* (New York: Houghton Mifflin Company, 1885). See: http://books.google.com/books?id =Xx5EAQAAIAAJ&printsec=frontcover&dq=Congressional+Government+wilso n&hl=en&ei=tOnDTqz6OOft0gHH3eyXDw&sa=X&oi=book_result&ct=result &resnum=1&ved=0CDQQ6AEwAA#v=onepage&q&f=false.

10 Thomas Jefferson to Edward Carrington, Paris, May 27, 1788. See: http://www.monticello.org/site/jefferson/natural-progress-things-quotation and http://memory.loc.gov/cgi-bin/ampage?collId=mtj1&fileName=mtj1pa ge009.db&recNum=456.

11 Ronald Reagan, Commencement Address, Eureka College, June 7, 1957. See: http://www.pbs.org/wgbh/americanexperience/features/primary-resources /reagan-eureka/.

12 Alexander Hamilton, "Federalist No. 33: The Same Subject Continued: Concerning the General Power of Taxation," from the *Daily Advertiser*. Published on December 26, 1787, under the pseudonym Publius. See: http://thomas.loc. gov/home/histdox/fed_28.html.

13 After reviewing hundreds of usages of "right" and "power" from the Founding Era, I have only discovered one instance in which a right may have been implied as belonging to a Government, and that is in Article 2 of the Articles of Confederation.

In that instance, it is not a direct assertion that States possessed rights, but rather an instance where they were granting powers to the Confederation. It appears from the context, that out of an abundance of caution, the States made the point of saying that they were NOT delegating any "sovereignty, freedom . . . independence . . . power, jurisdiction, [and] *right*" unless the Confederation "expressly delegated [it] to the United States, in Congress assembled." Interestingly, other than the Preamble, this sentence also contains the only use of the word state (with a lowercase s) out of more than 130 uses in the document.

14 James Madison, "Federalist No. 45: The Alleged Danger from the Powers of the Union to the State Governments Considered," for the *Independent Journal.* Published on January 26, 1788, under the pseudonym Publius. See: http://thomas.loc.gov/home/histdox/fed_45.html.

15 Alexander Hamilton, "Federalist No. 28: The Same Subject Continued: The Idea of Restraining the Legislative Authority in Regard to the Common Defense Considered," for the *Independent Journal.* Published on December 26, 1787, under the pseudonym Publius. See: http://thomas.loc.gov/home/histdox/fed_28.html.

16 Woodrow Wilson, *Congressional Government.*

17 Ibid.

18 James Madison, Virginia Ratifying Convention, June 2, 1788. See: http://www.constitution.org/rc/rat_va_05.htm.

19 James Madison, *Letters and Other Writings of James Madison*, IV (Philadelphia: J. B. Lippincott & Co., 1865). Letter from James Madison to James Robertson, April 20, 1831.

20 Thomas Jefferson, "Jefferson's Opinion on the Constitutionality of a National Bank, 1791." See: http://avalon.law.yale.edu/18th_century/bank-tj.asp.

21 Ibid.

22 James Madison, Virginia Resolution, 1798. See: http://memory.loc.gov /cgi-bin/ampage?collId=lled&fileName=004/lled004.db&recNum=539.

23 James Madison, Report on the Virginia Resolutions, 1800. See: http://memory.loc.gov/cgi-bin/ampage?collId=lled&fileName=004 /lled004.db&recNum=557.

24 James Madison, "Import Duties, House of Representatives," April 9, 1789, Document 18. See: http://press-pubs.uchicago.edu/founders/documents/a1_8_1s18.html.

25 Woodrow Wilson, *Congressional Government.*

26 Here we are considering the Government as a whole. There are now, and always have been, Constitutional Patriots within the government who fight for freedom and against tyranny. They are now, and usually have been, at best a small but vocal minority.

27 Woodrow Wilson, *Congressional Government.*

28 Thomas Jefferson, "Preamble to a Bill for the More General Diffusion of

Knowledge," Fall 1778, Document 11. See: http://press-pubs.uchicago.edu/founders/documents/v1ch18s11.html.

29 Thomas Jefferson, First Inaugural Address, March 4, 1801. See: http://www.princeton.edu/~tjpapers/inaugural/infinal.html.

30 James Wilson, Pennsylvania Ratifying Convention, December 4, 1787, Document 5. See: http://press-pubs.uchicago.edu/founders/documents/a1_8_18s5.html.

31 Alexander Hamilton, "Federalist No. 33."

32 James Monroe, Virginia Ratifying Convention, June 10, 1788. See: http://www.constitution.org/rc/rat_va_08.htm.

33 See: http://www.law.duke.edu/shell/cite.pl?65+Law+&+Contemp.+Probs.+1+(Spring+2002).

34 The only exception is the 12th Amendment.

35 Until the States ratified the 17th Amendment in 1913, each State legislature chose its own Senators.

36 George Washington, Farewell Address.

37 Richard Stengel, "One Document, Under Siege," *Time* (July 4, 2011). See: http://www.time.com/time/nation/article/0,8599,2079445,00.html.

38 Philip Rucker and Krissah Thompson, "Two new rules will give Constitution a starring role in GOP-controlled House," *Washington Post* (December 30, 2010). See: http://www.washingtonpost.com/wp-dyn/content/article/2010/12/29/AR2010122901402.html?sid=ST2010122901409.

39 "S. Doc. 108-17—Acts of Congress Held Unconstitutional in Whole or in Part by the Supreme Court of the United States" (Washington, D.C.: U.S. Government Printing Office, 2002). According to this report, only 158 out of 1,539 laws struck down in 223 years have been Federal laws. See: http://www.gpo.gov/fdsys/search/pagedetails.action?na=&se=&sm=&flr=&ercode=&dateBrowse=&collection=&historical=false&st=Acts+of+Congress+Held+as+Unconstitutional&=Unconstitutional+and+Preempted+Laws+1789-2002&psh=&sbh=&tfh=&originalSearch=&granuleId=GPO-CONAN-2002-10&packageId=GPO-CONAN-2002a.

40 Woodrow Wilson, *Congressional Government*.

41 William F. Buckley, Mission Statement for the *National Review*, November 19, 1955. See: http://www.nationalreview.com/articles/223549/our-mission-statement/william-f-buckley-jr.

42 James Rees, *The Beauties of the Hon. Daniel Webster* (New York: J. and H. G. Langley, 1839). See: http://books.google.com/books?id=4ythIZ6mYfMC&printsec=frontcover&dq=beauties+of+the+hon.+daniel+webster&hl=en&ei=ZPXCTvKHN4Xd0QGHq42dDw&sa=X&oi=book_result&ct=result&resnum=1&ved=0CC4Q6AEwAA#v=onepage&q&f=false.

43 George Washington, First Inaugural Address, April 30, 1789. See: http://www.archives.gov/exhibits/american_originals/inaugtxt.html.

CONSTITUTION ENDNOTES

1 This is known as the "Elector (voter) Qualification Clause." The original says, "of the most numerous Branch of the State Legislature." At the time it was possible that voting requirements could be different from one branch to another. But as modified by various amendments, almost anyone over eighteen years of age can now vote in virtually any election. See **C:1.2.3a** and the several Amendments that affect it.

2 **Legislature** means any "group of lawmakers." In the Constitution, the term refers consistently to the lawmakers of one or more of the States, *not* to **Congress**. Congress is first mentioned by saying it will have "all *legislative* Powers herein granted" (**C:1.1.1**). But after that introduction, it is consistently called Congress, or when just one House is discussed, the **House of Representatives**, or the **Senate**. The Constitution frequently refers to Congress's power to *make law*, but never calls Congress a *legislature*.

3 Every reference to *he, him,* and *his* has been changed to gender-neutral or gender-inclusive terminology to show the effect of the 19th Amendment, which gave women the right to vote in 1920.

4 This Clause was superseded by Section 2 of the 14th Amendment, which has replaced nearly all of it here except for a few words concerning taxes, which the 14th Amendment did not address. The original text counted three-fifths of the slave population for both representation and taxation. This was known as the **three-fifths compromise**. In 1868, the 14th Amendment voided this formula, and added language about the right to vote. Several other Amendments expanded this right.

5 Under the original Constitution, all **direct taxes** had to be calculated in such a way that the amount each State paid was in proportion (apportioned) to its population (**C:1.9.4**). The 16th Amendment created an exception. See Amendment 16 and endnote 76.

6 This sentence incorporates the effects of the 15th, 19th, 24th, and 26th Amendments concerning race, gender, poll tax, and age.

7 When voters cast their ballots for President and Vice President, they are actually choosing **electors** from their State (or from Washington, D.C.). These electors, in turn, vote for President and Vice President, as described in **C:2.1**.

8 Congress determines the number of Representatives, provided that each State must have at least one, the number must be proportional to population, and there may not be more than one for every thirty thousand people. The number

of Representatives rose steadily until 1911, when it was fixed at 435, where it remains today. Nothing in the Constitution prevents Congress from changing the number in the future.

9   An **impeachment** is a formal *charge* of wrongdoing that can only be brought by the House of Representatives, as indicated here. The actual trial to determine *guilt* takes place in the Senate (**C:1.3.6–7**).

10 This paragraph is the modern version of the text of **A:17a**, which changed the method of electing Senators and added that States had to use the same voter (elector) qualifications for U.S. Senate elections as they were using for state legislature elections. (Until the 17th Amendment, Senators were elected by State Legislatures. After the 17th Amendment, they were chosen by popular vote, much like members of House.)

11 See **C:1.2.1** and endnotes 1 and 2.

12 This paragraph is the modern version of the text of **A:17b**, which modified the provisions for filling vacancies.

13 The person who **presides** over something, whether it is a corporation, college, bank, or government, is called the **president** of that entity (see endnote 15). In the Constitution, **President** refers to the chief executive of the United States (see Article 2). The person who would take over the President's duties if he or she dies, or becomes unable to continue in office, is called the **Vice President**. If the Vice President takes over, even temporarily, during that time, he or she is called the **Acting President**. The Vice President is also the **President of the Senate**. He or she **presides** over it much of the time. When he or she is not there, the **President Pro Tempore** presides (see endnote 14). The **President-elect** and **Vice President–elect** are individuals who have been elected, but have not yet had their terms begin or taken their oaths of office. See **C:1.4.2** and Amendment 20 and the endnotes for these items for more information on the time between elections and the beginnings of terms.

14 The original phrase here is **pro tempore**, which means "temporary," or "for the time."

15 According to *Noah Webster's 1828 American Dictionary of the English Language,* **preside** means "To be set over for the exercise of authority; to direct, control and govern, as the chief officer. A man may *preside* over a nation or province; or he may *preside* over a senate, or a meeting of citizens."

16 An impeachment is a formal *charge* of wrongdoing that can only be brought by the House of Representatives (**C:1.2.5**). The actual trial to determine *guilt* takes place in the Senate, as indicated here.

17 The original states, "they shall be on Oath or Affirmation." Before conducting an impeachment trial, the Senators take an oath to act impartially as if they were judges or jurors. Generally, people who object to taking an oath in any court

(often on religious grounds), may instead *affirm* that they will act impartially, or tell the truth, or whatever would have been expected if they had taken an oath.

18 For example, an official could be impeached if he or she was accused of murder (or some other serious crime). If the House of Representatives *impeached* that official, and the Senate *convicted* him or her, the most they could do remove the official from office, and ban him or her from future office. That would not let the official off the hook for the murder (or the other serious crime). He or she could, and most likely would, be arrested and tried by the proper authorities.

19 The original adds an exception for the *place* of choosing Senators. At the time, Senators were chosen by State legislatures, so it was important for States to retain autonomy over the place of those elections. The 17th Amendment changed the method of electing Senators to a popular election. There is no mention in the 17th Amendment of where the elections take place, or who has final authority to decide this, but it is likely a moot point and so it was left out of this version.

20 Some of this language is from the 20th Amendment, which took effect in 1933. Until then, the date that the **terms** of Congress began and ended were simply set by Law, not by the Constitution. For more information, see the 20th Amendment, Sections 1 and 2, and endnotes 80 and 81.

21 A **quorum** is the minimum number of persons that must be present for a group to conduct business. Often, as here, a majority is considered a quorum. But it can be a different number (**C:2.1.3d** and **2.1.3g**).

22 **Adjourn** means to end a meeting, usually with a plan to reconvene at a later time and/or in another place.

23 The language about the change in pay is from the 27th Amendment (1992), and is included here.

24 Courts have held that this protection generally extends only to civil arrests (which are virtually nonexistent today), not criminal arrests. This portion of the Clause may be obsolete for all practical purposes.

25 The original uses the phrase *general Welfare*. The meaning here has to do with the mutual well-being of all the member States. This usage can be seen more clearly in phrases from the Articles of Confederation, the agreement drafted by the Second Continental Congress in 1776–77 and ratified (approved) by the thirteen Founding States in 1781 (see endnote 56): "[the States] mutual and general welfare" and "for the defense and welfare of the United States, or any of them." *Noah Webster's 1828 American Dictionary* defines **welfare** as "Exemption from any unusual evil or calamity; the enjoyment of peace and prosperity, or the ordinary blessings of society and civil government; applied to states."

26 These kinds of taxes were considered **indirect**. The constitutional standard for **indirect taxes** was that they be *uniform* or consistent, the same everywhere. Contrast this with **direct taxes**, which had to be *apportioned*, or in proportion to population (**C:1.9.4**). The 16th Amendment allowed Congress to assess an income tax, which is a direct tax that is *not* based upon population. Until this Amendment was ratified in 1913, all direct taxes were required to be apportioned (**C:1.9.4**). Income tax also affected **C:1.2.3a**. This effect has been incorporated into the corresponding texts.

27 Section 1 of the 14th Amendment expanded this Power by defining citizenship and adding federal protection for the rights of citizens.

28 In the original, these letters of retaliation were called **Letters of Marque and Reprisal**. These letters were given by various governments to permit private citizens to do a number of things normally associated with the military, such as recover lost property or use force to get even with an enemy for damages. They were sometimes authorized to capture enemies and enemy ships.

29 *Captures* probably means property that was captured. But there is some evidence that the meaning might also include captured people, so it was not modernized, as any synonym might prejudice the meaning.

30 There is much discussion about the meaning of the term **Militia** as it has evolved over the years. But at the time that the Constitution was drafted and ratified, nearly all able-bodied men in any State were considered to be part of that State's Militia. They were expected to keep their own arms, and bring those arms with them to fight when needed, as they had just done during the Revolution. See also the 2nd Amendment and endnote 58.

31 The original doesn't mention Washington, D.C. (District of Columbia), since that District had not yet been selected. Washington, D.C. has been "the Seat of the Government of the United States" since 1800. See also Amendment 23 and endnote 85.

32 These are storage areas around a dock, especially for naval supplies.

33 This Section includes limits on taxing, lawmaking, and the United States Government in general. It also lists certain rights of citizens and State protections. There are substantial parallels to the Bill of Rights, which expands on the same concepts.

34 This was an oblique reference to the slave trade, which was protected by this compromise for about twenty years. At the first constitutionally permitted opportunity, a Federal Law banning all future slave trade was passed by Congress and signed by President Thomas Jefferson. It became effective on January 1, 1808. Slavery itself was abolished by the 13th Amendment in 1865. The whole Clause may be obsolete, but it was retained here because it was changed by Law, not repealed or replaced by Amendment. Some State authority regarding immigration in general may remain.

35 This right to be seen by a Judge to determine whether a person is being properly held is called a **writ of habeas corpus**. A writ is a written judicial order; the Latin

phrase *habeas corpus* literally means "you should have [produce] the body" and dates back to medieval British law.

36 This Clause prohibits any act of legislature that declares a person to be guilty of a crime and convicted without benefit of a judicial trial; such a Law is called a **bill of attainder**. Bills of attainder were part of British law from the fourteenth to the nineteenth centuries, and were often enacted against those accused of treason. These bills have a complex history, including cases where people were executed and their property confiscated. Under the Constitution, Congress can set the penalty for treason (**C:3.3.2**), but guilt is determined by the courts.

37 An **ex post facto Law**—the term used in the original Clause—is a retroactive Law. *Ex post facto* means "done after the fact" (the literal Latin translation is "from a thing done afterward"). So, Congress may not decide that something *should have been* a crime and make a Law that is effective retroactively to punish the person(s) who did it.

38 The Constitutional standard for **direct taxes** is that they be **apportioned**, meaning shared in proportion to each State's population. The income tax (allowed by the 16th Amendment in 1913) became the exception to that rule. See Amendment 16 and endnote 76.

39 Many other countries at the time of the drafting of the Constitution, including England, had classes of people. There were nobles of various ranks, such as duke, marquis, earl, viscount, and baron. These people were regarded as having a higher rank in society than the rest of the people, who were called "commoners."

40 Section 1 of the 14th Amendment contains additional prohibitions concerning what States may not do.

41 **Letters of Marque and Reprisal.** See **C:1.8.11** and endnote 28.

42 **Bills of attainder.** See **C:1.9.3** and endnote 36.

43 **Ex post facto Laws.** See **C:1.9.3** and endnote 37.

44 The original does not set any limit on the number of terms a President may serve. Since 1951, the 22nd Amendment has limited Presidents to being *elected* to two terms. It also allows for them to have previously served up to two years of someone else's term. See the 22nd Amendment for more detail.

45 The original does not establish the beginning and ending of the President's term. This was simply set by Law as March 4 until 1933, when the 20th Amendment changed it to January 20 and made it part of the Constitution. Federal election dates are still set by Law, and are presently the Tuesday after the first Monday in November in even-numbered years. A President is elected in every other Federal election, so if a year is divisible by four, there will be a presidential election that year in November. The President will take office at noon on January 20 of the following year.

46 Originally, only the States appointed electors. In 1961, the 23rd Amendment gave Washington, D.C. the right to appoint some electors. For details, see **A:23**, and endnote 85.

47 The next seven Clauses are the full text of the 12th Amendment, which superseded the original. The addition of these Clauses lengthens this section considerably over the original, and changes the numbering of the Clauses significantly. The method of electing the President was changed in 1804 by the 12th Amendment, and again in 1933 by the 20th Amendment. Clauses **2.1.3a** through **2.1.3g** are the full text of the 12th Amendment, *as amended by* the 20th Amendment. So there are actually two paragraphs that appear in this version three times: **C:2.1.3e–f, A:12.e–f,** and **A:20.3.a–b.**

48 **C:2.1.6a–b** and **C:2.1.6d–g** are the text of the 25th Amendment (1967). They supersede one simple paragraph in the original text about presidential succession. The addition of these Clauses lengthens this Section considerably over the original, and changes the numbering of the Clauses significantly.

49 This provision allows Congress to write Laws that determine who will be President if *both* the President and Vice President become unable to serve for any reason. The Law that currently determines this is called the Presidential Succession Act of 1947. Under this Law, the Speaker of the House of Representatives is next in line behind the Vice President, followed by the President Pro Tempore of the Senate, the Secretary of State, and the other members of the Cabinet.

50 The actual language reads "a majority of . . . the principal officers of the executive departments." These department heads are often referred to as the President's Cabinet or Cabinet officers.

51 Two provisions in this Clause were nullified in 1795 by the 11th Amendment, so they have been deleted here. Before the 11th Amendment, the Supreme Court also had authority over controversies between one State and citizens of a different State, and also between a State (or its citizens) and a foreign State (or its citizens).

52 The original uses the phrase **work corruption of blood**. Under **common law** (see Amendment 7 and endnote 63), traitors would be executed and their property would then be confiscated. This also had the effect of punishing the traitor's heirs, or bloodline.

53 **General Laws** are uniform from State to State, not specific to a certain case.

54 The original had a Clause about returning slaves who escaped. This was nullified by the 13th Amendment in 1865, so that Clause is deleted here.

55 In this paragraph, various forms of the word *approve* replace various forms of the word *ratify*, which appears in the original.

56 The **Confederation** was the arrangement the States operated under before this Constitution was ratified (approved) in 1789. The **Articles of Confederation** was the agreement between the States that served much the same function as the Constitution. It was under this agreement that the **Confederacy** actually became known as the **United States of America**. The Articles of Confederation was drafted by the Second Continental Congress in 1776–77 and ratified (approved) by all thirteen States in 1781, all while they were fighting the Revolutionary War. The framers of the Constitution met in Philadelphia in 1787 for the purpose of **amending** these **Articles**, and ended up drafting a brand new agreement. Here (**C:6.1**), the framers are reaffirming all debts and agreements made while they were operating under the **Articles of Confederation**.

57 These first ten Amendments of the Constitution were proposed and ratified as a group. Some States refused to ratify the Constitution unless this **Bill of Rights** was promised. Twelve Amendments were originally proposed by Congress; these ten were ratified effective December 15, 1791. One, concerning Congressional pay raises, was ratified over two hundred years later as the 27th Amendment.

58 The original uses the term *arms,* which includes firearms and other military weapons.

59 For a definition of **Militia**, see **C:1.8.15** and endnote 30.

60 The original calls this reasonable belief **probable cause**. Just how *probable* the *cause* has to be for a warrant to be issued has been the subject of many court cases.

61 The original uses the phrase **Oath or affirmation**. People who object to making a statement under *oath* (often on religious grounds) may instead *affirm* that they are telling the truth.

62 This sentence only affected serious crimes in 1791. But in modern practice, this principle of "double jeopardy" has been extended by the courts to include all, or nearly all, crimes. This has had the effect of *increasing* the protection guaranteed by this Amendment.

63 **Common law** is a big subject. But a short definition is that it is the body of law based on customs and previous cases that were decided through the court system as opposed to the legislature; the concept of common law, which dates back to medieval England, is part of many legal systems in countries all over the world.

64 While some of the founders would not support the Constitution without a Bill of Rights, others opposed it on the grounds that listing a few of their rights might cause their other rights to be "denied or disparaged." The 9th Amendment was included to address this concern.

65 The list of Powers that the United States Government *does have* is contained in the Constitution. They are often referred to as **enumerated**, or listed, Powers. Most of them are summarized in **C:1.8**. The list of powers the States *do not have* is also contained in the Constitution. Most of these are listed in **C:1.10**.

66 The effect of the 11th Amendment on **C:3.2** has already been incorporated into the text of that Section.

67 The 12th Amendment substantially affected **C:2.1**, superseding much of the original language. As a result, the entire Amendment has been duplicated and inserted into this version as **C:2.1.3a–g**.

68 The next two Sections are actually **A:20.3.a–b**, which superseded one sentence in the original.

69 The effect of the 13th Amendment on **C:4.2.2** has already been incorporated into the text of that Clause. See also **C:1.9.1** and endnote 34.

70 Section 1 of the 14th Amendment has the effect of adding new power for the United States to define citizenship and protect the freedoms of citizens (see **C:1.8.4**). It also limits what States may do as listed in **C:1.10**. Section 2 superseded **C:1.2.3a**, and has already been duplicated and added there, virtually replacing that Clause except for a few words concerning taxes.

71 This sentence also incorporates the effects of the 15th, 19th, 24th, and 26th Amendments concerning race, gender, poll tax, and age.

72 When voters cast their ballots for President and Vice President, they are actually choosing **electors** from their State (or from Washington, D.C.). These electors, in turn, vote for President and Vice President, as described in **C:2.1**.

73 This Section was designed to disqualify people who had held certain offices and then participated in the Civil War on the side of the South.

74 This Section affirms all debts incurred by the North in the Civil War, but nullifies all debts incurred by the South.

75 The effect of the 15th Amendment on **A:14.2** and on **C:1.2.3a** has already been incorporated into those texts.

76 The 16th Amendment had the effect of adding a new Power of Congress like those listed in **C:1.8**. It also affected **C:1.2.3a** and **C:1.9.4**. The effect has been incorporated into those texts.

77 The effects of the 17th Amendment on **C:1.3.1** and **C:1.3.2b** have already been incorporated into those texts.

78 It is often said that the 21st Amendment **repealed**, or canceled out, the 18th Amendment, and Section 1 of the 21st Amendment says just that. But Section 2 of the 21st Amendment then offers new language that has Federal implications for violating State Laws concerning the transporting and importing of alcoholic beverages.

79 The effect of the 19th Amendment on **A:14.2**, and on **C:1.2.3a** has already been incorporated into those texts.

80 Section 1 of the 20th Amendment establishes the **terms** for President, Vice President, Senators, and Representatives. The effect on the President's term was incorporated into **C:2.1.1**. (The President's term was restated for clarity in **A:20.3** of this version.)

81 Section 2 of the 20th Amendment establishes the first **meeting** date of Congress in each year. Sections 1 and 2 affected **C:1.4.2** and the effects have been incorporated there. Until the 20th Amendment took effect in 1933, the date that the **terms** of Congress and the President began and ended were simply set by Law, not by the Constitution. From the beginning, Congress set that date as March 4. The Constitution set their first *meeting* date as "the first Monday in December," so

nine months would elapse between the start of the Congressional *term* and their first *meeting*. A few more months would elapse between Federal *elections* and the start of the *term*. So a full year could elapse between the *elections* and the first *meeting*. Because of the 20th Amendment, there is a much shorter time between Congressional elections and the date their terms begin. Their first meeting is now set for the same day as the start of their term. (The first meeting date, but not the date the term begins, may still be changed by Law). Similarly, the President's term now begins on January 20.

82 Section 3 of the 20th Amendment superseded Section 5 of the 12th Amendment. The 12th Amendment had already superseded several Clauses in Article 2, Section 1. The 12th Amendment, as amended by the 20th Amendment, is seen again in the modern version as **C:2.1.3a–g**. See **C:2.1.3a–g**, and Amendment 12, and endnotes 47 and 67.

83 The effect of this Amendment on **C:2.1.1** has already been incorporated into the text of that Clause.

84 The effect of this Amendment on **C:2.1.2** has already been incorporated into the text of that Clause.

85 The original calls Washington, D.C. "the District constituting the seat of Government of the United States."

86 The effect of this Amendment on **A:14.2**, and on **C:1.2.3a** has already been incorporated into those texts.

87 See endnote 7 and **C:2.1** regarding electors.

88 This Amendment substantially affected **C:2.1**, superseding some of the original language. As a result, the entire Amendment has been duplicated and inserted into this version as **C:2.1.6a–b** and **C:2.1.6d–g**.

89 The actual language says "a majority of . . . the principal officers of the executive departments." These department heads are often referred to as the President's Cabinet or Cabinet officers.

90 The effects of this Amendment on **A:14.2** and **C:1.2.3a** have already been incorporated into those texts.

91 This Amendment affected **C:1.6.1a**, and the effects have been incorporated into that text. It was proposed as one of the original Bill of Rights, but it was not approved until over two hundred years later, which was possible because there was no deadline set for ratification. Some more recent Amendments have set seven-year deadlines for ratification.

RECOMMENDED RESOURCES

Many of these resources are available online and in print. There are many others that can be easily found online using any standard search engine.

Blackstone, Sir William, *Commentaries on the Laws of England.* Oxford: Clarendon Press, 1765–69.
(Available online at the Avalon Project of Yale Law School: http://avalon.law.yale.edu/subject_menus/blackstone.asp)
For the very serious student who wishes to understand the fundamentals of English law, which provided much of the legal framework and background that the framers of the Constitution would have been familiar with.

Farrand, Max, ed. *The Records of the Federal Convention of 1787.* New Haven: Yale University Press, 1911. 3 vols.
(A 1911 version is available at the Online Library of Liberty: http://oll.libertyfund.org/index.php?option=com_staticxt&staticfile=show.php ?title=1785&Itemid=27)
This lengthy work is also a resource for the serious student, but anyone can enjoy perusing excerpts. Includes the notes of James Madison, which have also been published separately. A later "Supplement" to these records is also available from Yale University Press.

Hamilton, Alexander, James Madison, and John Jayl. *The Federalist.* Benjamin Fletcher Wright, Ed. New York: Barnes & Noble, 2004.
(An 1818 version is available at the Online Library of Liberty: http://oll.libertyfund.org/index.php?option=com_staticxt&staticfile=show.php %3Ftitle=788&Itemid=27)
This is a standard volume for students of the Constitution. One or more versions are available at most bookstores. Contains the arguments of Alexander Hamilton, James Madison, and John Jay as they wrote (under the collective pseudonym of "Publius") in favor of ratifying the new Constitution.

Hirsch, E.D. *Validity in Interpretation.* New Haven: Yale University Press, 1967.
A standard work on the principles of literary interpretation.

Ketcham, Ralph, ed. *The Anti-Federalist Papers and the Constitutional Convention Debates.* New York: New American Library, 2003.

(Similar information is available online at http://www.constitution.org/afp/afp.htm)
This collection is reader friendly and includes many of the best portions of the larger compilations by Farrand and Storing.

Meese III, Edwin, Matthew Spalding, and David Forte, eds. *The Heritage Guide to the Constitution.* Washington, D.C.: Regnery Publishing Company, 2005.
This is an almost line-by-line commentary on the Constitution from a number of contributors who generally observe the Originalist perspective. Relevant court cases are also frequently cited and discussed.

Storing, Herbert J., and Murray Dry, eds. *The Complete Anti-Federalist.* Chicago: University of Chicago Press, 1981.
Several American patriots gave speeches and wrote articles opposing the approval of the new Constitution, believing that the Articles of Confederation were sufficient for an alliance of independent States. These writers generally wrote under pseudonyms, but included Patrick Henry and other well-known figures of the Revolution. Storing also published an excerpted version in 1985, called simply, *The Anti-Federalist.*

Story, Joseph. *Commentaries on the Constitution of the United States.* Boston: Hilliard, Gray and Company, 1833.
(Available online at The Constitution Society: www.constitution.org/js/js_000.htm)

Webster, Noah. *American Dictionary of the English Language 1828.* Chesapeake, VA: FACE Publishing, 1968.
(Online word searches available at: http://1828.mshaffer.com/)
This dictionary was published forty-one years after the drafting of the Constitution and captures the meaning of the words as they were used at the time more closely than later dictionaries.

ACKNOWLEDGMENTS

I am grateful to the various Tea Parties, 912 groups, and the host of other freedom troops for the reception they have given to me and the self-published version of this book at so many events. That great response is truly what led Sterling to publish this new edition. I am indebted to the whole cast and crew of the Tea Party Express for welcoming me as one of their own. We are all family now, but two special men stand out.

Kristofer Pagard has been my assistant on three national tours and many local events. He is a true patriot and the most cheerful, loyal, and hard-working companion that I could have prayed for. He routinely anticipates my needs, promotes me with exuberance, and even makes allowance for my moods. A month at a time on the road (with long days and short nights) sometimes brought out my worst, and then Kristofer's best.

Howard Kaloogian, chairman of the political action committee that does business as Tea Party Express, believed in me from the first, granted me precious stage time, and put my book front and center at every event. He also introduced me to his long-time friend, former Attorney General Ed Meese, who then graciously agreed to write the foreword for this edition.

Ed Meese. Words fail me. "Thank you" does not approach my appreciation. "Honored" get closer.

Many thanks to best-selling author Tom Woods, who encouraged me to seek out a major publisher, then introduced me to his own agent, Andrew Stuart, who in turn presented my script to Sterling Publishing. It was there that Barbara Berger patiently edited and improved every portion of the manuscript. Each of these people took a chance on me that I trust this present work will reward.

Dennis Cheaqui of Great Divide Printing and Graphics not only designed and printed the earlier version of this book, he manned the home front every time I went on tour. Dennis cheerfully shipped books and supplies ahead of the tour buses with never a charge except the debt of friendship. He is also the man my wife leans on when her man is far away.

My wife, Cathy, has been my partner in every crime for nearly thirty years. We have raised (and are raising) seven children together in our "sweet Rocky Mountain paradise." My life without writing or speaking would still be everything a man could hope for. But a life without my bride would not be worth owning, and is beyond the farthest frontier of my deepest fear. It seems almost trivial to mention that she also guarded my work time, offered valuable critiques, and managed shipping.

Our younger children (Levi, Mary, and AmyJoy) have been very patient with the events that I have missed and the outings that have been postponed. They understand that the price of freedom is something that families sometimes pay together, and that our sacrifice pales in comparison to our men and women in uniform, and the families who pray for their safe return. Our family prays with them and for them every night of the world, even if Daddy is on a cell phone.

INDEX

Note: Abbreviations such as C:1.8 follow the shorthand numbering system described on page xv to indicate Constitution Articles and Sections. Numbers in parentheses, e.g. (17), indicate the number of an Amendment to the Constitution. Pages with n symbols (113n57) are pages with footnotes. The number following the page indicates the footnote number.